WHITE GARDENS

Creating Magnificent Moonlit Spaces

Guide to WHITE and LUMINOUS PLANTS

By Nina Koziol

This book is dedicated to my English mum, Terry.

White Gardens: Creating Magnificent Moonlit Spaces
Managing Editor: Gretchen Bacon
Editor: Joseph Borden
Copy Editor: Kurt Connelly
Designer: Mary Ann Kahn
Indexer: Jay Kreider

ISBN: 978-1-58011-580-3

Library of Congress Control Number: 9781580115803

We are always looking for talented authors. To submit an idea, please send a brief inquiry to acquisitions@foxchapelpublishing.com.

Printed in China
First Printing

Creative Homeowner®, *www.creativehomeowner.com*, is an imprint of New Design Originals Corporation and distributed exclusively in North America by Fox Chapel Publishing Company, Inc., 800-457-9112, 903 Square Street, Mount Joy, PA 17552, and in the United Kingdom by Grantham Book Service, Trent Road, Grantham, Lincolnshire, NG31 7XQ.

Contents

Part One

Part Two

Background & Highlights

Selecting the Plants

Introduction

*"And still within a summer's night
A something so transporting bright,
I clap my hands to see."*

—Emily Dickinson (1830-1886)

The Joy of an Evening Garden

The reclusive American poet Emily Dickinson was devoted to gardening and no doubt spent evenings wandering her family's gardens and meadows in Amherst, Massachusetts, looking for inspiration. She was keenly interested in all nature had to offer, from blossoms and birds to beetles and butterflies. Her poems illustrate how attuned she was to the weather, the changing seasons, and transitions in the garden throughout the day and into night.

Dickinson appreciated that a garden with white flowers at night is totally different from one enjoyed during the day. On sunny days, we tend to appreciate showy, vibrant hues—the bright reds, oranges, blues and purples—of annuals, perennials, shrubs, and vines. By late afternoon or early evening, as the sun begins to set, those glorious colors fade. Orange and red become muted, and deep colors disappear in the darkness. Evening is the time when shimmering

Like crepe paper, the petals of tree peony flowers reflect the light at dusk and beyond.

white blossoms and silver or variegated foliage become the stars of the garden. While understated during the day, white, lemon-yellow, and the palest pink flowers appear to glow at night, reflecting ambient light. This is when the white garden, also known as the evening garden or moon garden, comes into its own. At sunset and beyond, the garden is transformed into something soothing, fragrant, and mysterious.

This book is a practical guide to creating your own white garden, whether your space is a condo with a balcony, a small urban lot, or a sweeping suburban property. New to gardening? All the basics—from soil preparation and plant selection to fertilizing and watering—are included so that your new white garden is a success. And for avid gardeners and landscape pros, White Gardens can take your projects up a notch with ideas for elegant, stunning designs.

Read it from cover to cover or use the book as a starting point for choosing and combining plants. The book is divided into two parts: "Background and Highlights" and "Selecting the Plants." The fascinating history of evening gardens, dating back several centuries and across the continents, begins in Chapter 1. The key components behind the white garden—from choosing a site and creating a succession of interest through the growing season—are covered in Chapter 2. The garden's "bones" or hardscape appear in Chapter 3, where you'll discover elements like fire features to warm the evening, water to reflect moonlight on clear nights, and lighting. You'll learn how to determine the right size for a patio or seating area and embellish your outdoor space with arbors and trellises—all important, long-lasting elements that can add value to your property. Selecting an appropriate spot for your white garden, whether you have sun, shade or some of both, is found in Chapter 4.

A bounty of design ideas for beds, borders, foundation plantings and containers are featured in Chapter 5. You can effectively combine plants so that they look interesting during the day and in the evening when you understand how color, texture, shape, and form work together (Chapter 6). When it comes to selecting plants, including those with fragrance, Chapters 7 through 11 offer a wealth of choices—from spring- and summer-blooming bulbs to annuals, perennials, shrubs, vines, and tropicals.

As bright colors fade at sunset, white flowers begin to glow.

Time spent in the garden at night is a sensuous experience. It helps you slow down while you look at the shadows cast by moonlight. There's the delicate tracery from branches and tree limbs cast onto the patio or lawn. When a gentle breeze floats by on a warm evening, you may catch a hint of vanilla or honey fragrance from sweet alyssum or tobacco flowers. Sit, watch, and listen. As night falls, we become much more attuned to our surroundings through scent and sound.

Some flowers emit a fragrance only after dusk. They have evolved to attract night-flying pollinators that navigate by scent. There are the delicate, fragrant flowers of jasmine, white roses, lilies, and petunias to enjoy. And there's the moonflower vine, clambering up an arbor or fence and twirling open its brilliant white blossoms as the sun sets.

The sounds at night also capture our attention more so than during the day. The soothing trickle of a fountain, the bell-like notes of wind chimes, or the rustle of leaves allows us to experience the garden in a totally different and captivating way.

By the summer solstice in June, many evening gardens are alive with magic and wonder. In some areas, fireflies slowly rise from beds, borders, and lawns like floating lanterns. Birdsong at dusk, the great chorus of insects serenading potential mates, the night sky, moths flitting amongst flowers—all of these help redirect our attention from the day's hustle to something ethereal and relaxing.

Part 1

Background & Highlights

There's much to be said for taking a stroll among your plants on a summer's eve at dusk. The concept of white gardens isn't just a contemporary trend; it's rooted deeply in history. The beauty of a white garden is that you can create one anywhere, in any part of the country with plants suited to your climate and terrain, whether it be in sun or shade. From its historic origins to the benefits it offers, like the way the white hues shimmer in the moonlight and provide a tranquil evening experience, there's a richness to these gardens that goes beyond aesthetics. It can be a small corner of an urban lot or a sweeping border in the suburbs. Planted near a front entry, a white-flowering moon garden is a delightful evening greeting for you and your visitors. A white garden can be as simple as a planted window box or containers placed around a door, a gate, or at the head of a path. The possibilities are endless and deeply rooted in tradition.

Let's get started!

Chapter 1

White Gardens
& Moonlight Gardens:
Past & Present

"Speak not—whisper not;
Here bloweth thyme and bergamot;
Softly on the evening hour,
Secret herbs their spices shower,
Dark-spiked rosemary and myrrh,
Lean-stalked, purple lavender . . . "

—*"The Sunken Garden," Walter de la Mare (1873-1956)*

Fragrant white phlox begins to glow as the sun sets.

Evening gardens and moonlight excursions have been popular for more than a thousand years. The moon's reflection on water has long been admired in Japan. During Japan's Heian Period (794-1185), the aristocracy held moon-viewing celebrations at harvest time. They would glide along in boats to welcome the arrival of the full moon while enjoying its reflection on the water's surface.

In Asia, a common garden theme is the perception and enjoyment of the moon. The Hirosawa Pond and Osawa Pond in Japan are remnants of Heian period gardens. The Hirosawa Pond was constructed as part of a temple garden built by the grandson of Emperor Uta. The pond is featured in many Japanese poems. The landscape boasts cherry trees, Japanese maples and willows, and is a popular spot for moongazing. Visitors enjoy the moon rising over the Higashiyama mountains, which are reflected in the water. When the weather conditions are right, the moon appears as a giant glowing disk over the mountain range.

The Osawa Pond is a manmade water feature in Kyoto next to Daikaku-ji Temple. This pond is the oldest known surviving part of any garden in Japan. Emperor Saga ordered its creation during his reign (809-823) or shortly after, and it was part of the garden while he resided in the temple. Today, visitors experience the garden from the veranda, but also while sailing on the pond in early autumn to view the harvest moon.

Taj Mahal's Moonlight Garden

The Emperor Shah Jahan built a Moonlight Garden (Mehtab Bagh) in Agra, India, between 1631 and 1635 where he could view the Taj Mahal, a gleaming white marble mausoleum he dedicated to his wife, Mumtaz Mahal. On moonlit nights the building is magnificently reflected in the pool and the Yamuna

Bird's eye view of the Taj Mahal at Agra.

River, producing an ethereal effect. The original garden was planted with fragrant flowers and used in the cool of the night. However, it was situated on a flood plain and deep silt eventually covered the grounds. Archeologists have unearthed evidence of some of the original plants including a sample of a champa tree. Related to magnolias, this tree produces large, fragrant flowers that bloom at night.

Indian Hill Farm in Massachusetts

One of the earliest recorded white gardens in the United States was that of Major Benjamin Perley Poore (1820-1887), a prominent American newspaper correspondent, editor, and author. His parents owned Indian Hill Farm, a 400-acre estate in Newburyport, Massachusetts. In 1831, they travelled extensively in England, taking their son Benjamin along. It's likely that they were influenced by the country's beautiful gardens and returned with many ideas.

At Indian Hill Farm, they laid out extensive gardens in 1833, including expansive double flower borders. During Major Poore's lifetime, the estate boasted a white garden

along with herds of white cows, flocks of white sheep, white oxen, white poultry, white pigeons, and a white dog. One might say he was a bit eccentric. A gentleman farmer and avid horticulturist, he planted many trees and designed extensive terraces, formal gardens, and intricate cart paths throughout the property.

Alice Morse Earle described Poore's garden in her book, *Old Time Gardens* (1901), writing, "I saw this lovely farmstead and radiant white garden first in glowing sunlight, but far rarer must have been its charm in moonlight…"

Behind Poore's enormous and ever-expanding mansion, the white garden

Alice Morse Earle detailed Poore's white garden in her book.

stretched up the hillside. The borders were edged with white-flowered candytuft. The spring palette included white daffodils, spring snowflake (*Leucojum vernum*), Star of Bethlehem, white-flowered shrubs like bridal-wreath spirea, deutzia and sweet-scented mock orange, as well as white-flowered cherry trees. Fragrant honeysuckle vines covered arches over the path.

Poore's white garden once boasted formal parterres at the top of the hill, but they were gone by 1901. Nevertheless, Earle was enchanted by her visit:

> This lovely garden, varied in shape, and extending in many and diverse directions and corners, bears as its crown a magnificent double flower border over seven hundred feet long.
>
> But the White Garden, ah! Then the garden truly lived; it was like lightest snow wreaths bathed in silvery moonshine with every radiant flower adoring the moon with wide-open eyes, and pouring forth incense at her altar. And it was peopled with shadowy forms shaped of pearly mists and dews; and white night moths bore messages for them from flower to flower—this garden then was the garden of my dreams.

Victorian Theme Gardens

White and assorted blooms against a Victorian brick backdrop create a timeless, refined aesthetic.

Monochromatic gardens rely on the use of one flower color, such as an all-white or all-blue garden. This type of garden was particularly popular with the Victorians in the late 1800s. At that time, the white garden was often called a moon garden because they found that white flowers and silver or green-and-white foliage at dusk seemed to glow in the fading light.

An illustration from the 1888 Vaughan's Seed catalog, published in Chicago, features a young woman in a long, white dress standing in a moon garden, surrounded by moonflower vine, caladium, and white dahlias. In 1889, Vaughan's Seed catalog promoted their seeds of moonflower vine, telling readers that "hundreds of thousands are sold yearly" and that the "demand sometimes exceeds the supply."

Fragrance was very important to the Victorians, as well. The cover of *Ladies' Home Journal* from June 1896 features a young woman enjoying the scent of white roses as she knelt in a border filled with carnations and irises. The rising sun behind her depicts the silhouette of a rugosa rose, recently introduced at that time from Japan to the United States.

An 1896 cover of *Ladies' Home Journal* depicts a woman taking in the scent of white roses.

Many seed companies began importing lilies from Japan in the 1890s. This charming illustration emphasizes the garden at night.

A cover from the 1890s magazine *Gardening*, published in Chicago, shows a porch draped in sweet autumn clematis and climbing nasturtiums.

For one dollar, gardeners could receive 25 different seed packets in the Night-Blooming Collection featured in John Gardiner's 1890 seed catalog.

Victorians embraced weeping plants like this panicle hydrangea, which has been trained as a small tree.

The night-blooming, fragrant tobacco flower was a Victorian gardener's favorite.

By the Light of the Moon

The moon has played a big role in food gardening since ancient times. People around the world have sown seeds by watching the moon's waxing and waning phases and using those events as a planting calendar. The idea is that water in the soil and in plants is affected by the gravitational pull of the moon, as are the tides. The tides are highest during the new and full phases of the moon and the theory is that seeds will absorb the most water during these times.

In the March 1913 issue of *Country Life in America*, a monthly periodical, the article "In the Dark O' The Moon" by Ida M. H. Starr focused on planting according to the moon's phases. She wrote:

> [A moon garden is] a place where flowers that love the night, azure, white, silver gray, and lavender—ghost flowers—bloom; where it is always still and peaceful; where no one ever hurries; where you wait for the moon to tell you the time to do things; where all manner of powers that people ordinarily do not consider, float down from the stars to make things grow; where the gardener hears wonderful sounds stealing down from the milky way, for he has time to listen you know; where Venus, Mars, Jupiter, Saturn and all the planets work together to help.

While few studies have been done to test the veracity of lunar gardening, it's a pleasant thought to be in the garden, planting by moonlight.

A White Garden in Wales

In her book *My Garden,* published in 1916, Louise Beebe Wilder (1878-1938) described a white garden she visited on the River Ely, not far from Llandaff in Wales:

> We saw this garden first at twilight, that witching hour, and through the tall iron gates, above which swung a clematis starred with immense white blooms, the effect was almost as if a mist had crept up from the river and finding the haven of this quiet enclosure had swirled around and about, rising here in wraith spires and turrets, lying there in gauzy breadths amidst the muted green. It is impossible to describe its beauty at this dim hour—so soft, so ethereal, so mysterious, half real it seemed.

Helena Rutherfurd Ely's 1916 book features white-flowered foxgloves on the cover.

Stately hollyhocks in white and yellow, single and double flowers from Peter Henderson's 1903 seed catalog.

Ellen Biddle Shipman (1869-1950).

Mina Edison's Moonlight Garden

American landscape architect Ellen Biddle Shipman designed a moonlight garden in 1929 for Mina and Thomas Edison in Fort Meyers, Florida (now the Edison & Ford Winter Estates). Mina envisioned a space for entertaining and Shipman included a pool for the moon's reflection. The Moonlight Garden is the largest garden on the site and the primary flower colors are white and blue, including queen's wreath (*Petrea volubilis*) and gardenias. Towering ficus trees planted by Thomas Edison, Henry Ford, and Harvey Firestone stand tall. Today, the Moonlight Garden provides an intimate, romantic setting filled with fragrant flowers and tall bougainvillea-entwined trellises and is used for weddings and other events.

Honey-scented sweet autumn clematis rambles over this fence in late summer.

The White Garden at Sissinghurst

Perhaps the most famous white garden is that of Vita Sackville-West, an English writer and gardener who, with her husband, diplomat and author Sir Harold Nicolson, lived at Sissinghurst Castle in Kent, England. In her weekly article for the Observer newspaper, Sackville-West told readers about her latest garden projects. In January 1950, she wrote of her plans for an evening garden, "I cannot help hoping that the great ghostly barn-owl will sweep silently across a pale garden, next summer in the twilight—the pale garden that I am now planting, under the first flakes of snow."

At that time, her magnificent property featured a cottage garden where she experimented with "hot" colors: orange, red, and yellow. She recognized that by restricting the new garden to white, silver, and gray, she needed to create interest and drama by using plants with contrasting shapes, heights, textures, and form. Her husband created the overall structure with dark green hedges of yew and boxwood. Her plans portrayed "a low sea of grey clumps of foliage, pierced here and there with tall white flowers."

Today, this world-renowned garden is filled with white-flowered roses, peonies, irises, hydrangeas, Japanese anemones, low mounds of silvery lamb's ears, silver artemisia, and santolina. Spires of foxtail lily (*Eremurus*), lilies, and verbascum punctuate the billowy flowers of *Ammi majus*. The star of the garden is the weeping silver-leaved pear tree, *Pyrus salicifolia* 'Pendula', a stunning and graceful focal point.

A white garden at Sissinghurst Castle.

Sissinghurst Castle's boxwood hedges enclose the white beds.

The Queen Anne's lookalike, *Ammi majus*, used at Sissinghurst.

Silver foliage contrasts with white flowers at Sissinghurst Castle.

Evening Gardens Today

Many public and private gardens feature beds, borders, and garden rooms filled with plants that can be enjoyed in the evening. At High Point University in High Point, North Carolina, the Mariana H. Qubein Arboretum & Botanical Gardens has a moon garden in the courtyard of the R.G. Wanek Center. The border includes many plants that boast white or pale flowers and fragrance or foliage that is showcased at night. Annual four-o'clocks open their flowers in the late afternoon to release a honey fragrance. The pendulous flowers of tropical *Brugmansia* (angel's trumpet) deliver their powerful scent after dusk. Woody plants, like weeping Japanese apricot trees, have subtle lighting to enhance their dramatic form at night.

At Kensington Palace in England, a white garden was planted in 2017 as a memorial to Princess Diana. This sweeping floral tribute contains white roses, cosmos 'Cupcakes White', and Gaura 'Belleza® White', along with white daffodils, tulips, sweet peas, phlox, lupines, peonies, and the very fragrant Koreanspice viburnum.

Koreanspice and Judd viburnums offer spring beauty and a sweet vanilla fragrance.

An evening garden today offers a respite from electronic devices, the nonstop news cycle, and the stress of everyday life. It's your opportunity to recharge and refocus on what's important. Let's look next at the elements that can help you create your own piece of evening paradise.

Candles give this contemporary white garden an added evening glow.

A peaceful evening garden filled with astilbe, hydrangeas, and a reflecting pool.

White petunias offer season-long bloom in containers and in the ground.

Caladium and silver-leaved *Pulmonaria* brighten the shade garden at dusk and beyond.

Roses offer fragrance in the sunny garden.

Gallery

In May, *Digitalis purpurea* 'Alba' sends up its flower spikes, while Dianthus 'Mrs. Sinkins' and *Centranthus ruber* 'Alba' are at their peak. Meanwhile, the round pond's first white water lilies begin to bloom. Photography by Jon Muñiz Elola, Lur Garden, Oiartzun, Spain.

The silvery soft foliage of lamb's ears (*Stachys byzantina*) serve as a counterpoint to the spiky blue fescues (*Festuca glauca*), while foxgloves and other white flowers provide vertical interest. Photography by Jon Muñiz Elola, Lur Garden, Oiartzun, Spain.

As August arrives, *Pennisetum macrourum* and *Pennisetum alopecuroides* display their light-catching spikes. All the while, *Gaura lindheimeri* continues its generous flowering. Photography by Jon Muñiz Elola, Lur Garden, Oiartzun, Spain.

July heralds the bloom of the Paniculata. Stars of the month are Hydrangea paniculata 'Phantom' and *Leucanthemum maximum*. Photography by Jon Muñiz Elola, Lur Garden, Oiartzun, Spain.

A blend of white fosteriana tulips such as *Tulipa* 'Purissima', 'White Valley', and 'Exotic Emperor' stand alongside the *Narcissus* 'Obdam'. A wall, draped in the delicate blooms of *Clematis armandii* 'Apple Blossom', completes the scene. Photography by Lena Knaus, The Garden Idea, Tagelswangen, Switzerland.

Clematis 'Huldine', with wreaths from last year's wood cuttings, intertwines gracefully with the *Rosa* 'Schneewalzer'. Photography by Lena Knaus, The Garden Idea, Tagelswangen, Switzerland.

A garden wall featuring *Rosa* 'Lykkefund', a rose that flowers once. Photography by Lena Knaus, The Garden Idea, Tagelswangen, Switzerland.

By day, the white garden accentuates the architectural grace of the house, its blooms and foliage creating a harmonious visual experience.

By night, strategic lighting enhances the garden's aesthetic appeal, the white blooms reflecting the soft light and emphasizing the architectural details.

Daisies, with their radiant white petals surrounding sunny yellow centers, epitomize the charm of nature's simplicity. Photography by Kate Van Druff, Bunny's Garden, Pennsylvania.

Petunia sp., commonly known as petunia, presents its white blooms, adding a straightforward and bright presence in gardens and containers. Photography by Kate Van Druff, Bunny's Garden, Pennsylvania.

A path lined with white flowers in the author's garden lights the way at dusk.

The pristine petals of white four o'clocks (*Mirabilis jalapa* 'Alba') open in the late afternoon, offering a nightly spectacle of beauty. Photography by Kate Van Druff, Bunny's Garden, Pennsylvania.

Mirabilis jalapa, showcasing a delicate hue of light pink to almost white, reveals its trumpet-shaped blooms. Photography by Kate Van Druff, Bunny's Garden, Pennsylvania.

Vinca sp., commonly known as periwinkle, features glossy green leaves paired with pristine white, star-shaped flowers, serving as both a decorative and functional ground cover. Photography by Kate Van Druff, Pennsylvania.

Kensington's White Garden boasts 4,000+ flowers: 200+ roses, 100 Forget-Me-Nots, 300+ tulips, 500+ lavender plants, 100+ dahlias, and roughly 50 sweet peas.

In 2017, the Sunken Garden at Kensington Palace was transformed into a white garden in memory of Princess Diana.

White Gardens

Annuals significantly enhance the growing season with their prolific blooming, offering a continual display of vibrant white flowers and enriching the garden's aesthetic appeal.

The fragrant flowers of Sweet Autumn clematis drape an arbor entry point in the author's garden.

White Gardens

A pergola leading into a white garden.

A single white bloom of *Petunia* sp. stands out, elegantly poised in its basket, adding a touch of simplicity to the setting.

A solitary white bloom of *Vinca* sp. shines brightly against its backdrop of glossy green leaves, highlighting its delicate beauty.

White mandevilla blooms glowing in the light of a super moon. Photography by Kate Van Druff, Bunny's Garden, Pennsylvania.

A cluster of Vinca sp. shines in the moonlight. Photography by Kate Van Druff, Bunny's Garden, Pennsylvania.

A single white zinnia glows in the light of a super moon. Photography by Kate Van Druff, Bunny's Garden, Pennsylvania.

These tall white garden phlox glow in the display beds at Walter's Gardens in Zeeland, Michigan.

The renowned white gardens at Sissinghurst exemplify meticulous design and horticultural excellence, reflecting Vita Sackville-West's vision. Each view reveals the thoughtful arrangement and diverse plant selection that continue to influence garden design today. Photography by Jonathan Buckley, Kent, England.

Anemone hybrida 'Honorine Jobert' in the early morning mist. Photography by Lena Knaus, The Garden Idea, Tagelswangen, Switzerland.

Chapter 2

Highlights of the White Garden: An Overview

"I love color, which I truly enjoy, but white is glorious forever."

—*Vita Sackville-West*

A white garden is attractive during the day, but it's especially lovely at dusk and beyond when the pale blossoms appear to glow. Who can resist luminous flowers like jasmine, roses, or lilies that are awash in fragrance? Certainly not the Victorians, who made the moonlight garden a favorite theme of the Gilded Age. Today, a shimmering white garden can complement any style house whether you live in a mid-century modern ranch, a Queen Anne-style home, an English-style Tudor, a bungalow, or a cottage.

A white garden can be contemporary, geometric, formal, or informal with winding borders like one you might see around a cottage or a farmhouse. It can be a white flowery meadow under an apple tree or two, or a sophisticated parterre—a rectangular boxwood hedge surrounding white-blooming roses or petunias. It all depends on your personal style, what you enjoy, and whether you will do the planting and maintenance or have help from a landscape contractor.

An elegant boxwood parterre filled with silver-leaved Dusty Miller glows at dusk in spring.

Fleece flower (*Persicaria polymorpha*) and variegated *Miscanthus* grass in Wisconsin are subtle in daylight and dazzling at dusk.

A white garden can complement any style home.

The Plant Palette

A garden filled with only white or the palest yellow and pink flowers is attractive because it conveys simplicity and elegance—it's subtle and calming. It's the total opposite of a border filled with flowers in vibrant reds, acid yellows, magenta, and vivid orange—colors that create excitement and exuberance during the day, but disappear at dusk. It's easy to make a wish list of white flowers you'd like to include because there are hundreds of plants to choose from and there is a white-flowering variety for many of them. There are white zinnias, marigolds, cosmos, dahlias, coneflowers, asters, lilies, liatris, salvia, butterfly bush, and countless others. If you like roses, there are many varieties available with fragrant white blossoms.

Flowers for the white garden may be creamy white, the palest yellow, pinkish-white, vanilla, muted white, or pristine white. They can have streaks of violet or pink or yellow at the center. Or they may have white ray petals with a green or burgundy cone in the center. Our eyes can detect the slightest difference in the shades of white so placement is important. For example, a murky white next to a crisp, bright white may make the former look very

This creamy white foxglove has bee guides—stripes and dots that direct pollinators to nectar.

dingy. This can be fixed by placing plants with interesting silver, gray or variegated foliage between them.

By the way, white (like black) is not a true color. A white surface reflects almost all the light rays and becomes the "color" with the greatest brightness. That's why anything white—from flowers and furniture to arbors and trellises—stands out in the shade and at night.

Pay attention to the different shades of white flowers. Murky white ageratum to the right of bright white petunias makes the former look dingy.

This white trellis-arbor combo will glow in the moonlight.

This lovely white garden is the perfect setting for an outdoor wedding.

A white patio set is far more visible in the evening than any other color.

Foliage Foils: Plants with Bright Leaves

Several cultivars of perennial forget-me-not (*Brunnera*) offer silver foliage.

Adding a Hint of Color

The white garden need not rely totally on white flowers. You can add a hint of color to create an interesting flower bed during the day. Small patches of light pink, pale yellow, or light blue flowers will lend a warm glow to a white border. However, a little bit of color goes a long way. Strong colors, such as red or orange, will quickly dominate the border.

White flowers serve as intermediaries between intense colors in a mixed-color border, especially in bright sunlight. Color preference is very personal. Some gardeners like cool colors—blue, violet, pink, purple, or mauve, while others prefer warm colors—red, orange, and yellow. Trust your own instinct when you visit other gardens or shop at the local garden center. Make notes of what catches your eye and take photos. The more white flowers you have, the more visible the garden will be in the evening.

Fun Foliage as Fillers

You can create a white garden by simply using white flowers, but it can be far more interesting if you include plants that have gray-green or silver leaves. Flowers can be fleeting, so that's when variegated, light-colored foliage comes to the rescue.

Since a white garden has a limited palette, the contrasts between leaf and flower shapes are important. For example, the silvery blue leaves of lavender make a nice foil for the glossy green leaves of white roses. The bright foliage of 'Silver Mound' *artemisia* and pale gray Dusty Miller play off white flowers and add to the overall mood.

The stark silvery white leaves of *Senecio candicans* Angel Wings® 'Senaw' (also known as Dusty Miller) reflect light and enhance the tiny flowers of Verbena.

Petunia grandiflora, known for its expansive blooms, is paired with the silvery leaves of Dusty Miller, offering a striking color and texture contrast in the flower bed.

Variegated perennial forget-me-nots (*Brunnera*) light up the ground plane under other plants and help separate conflicting shades of white.

For a rich visual effect, select plants with silver, white, or blue foliage, such as blue oat grass, blue fescue, blue-leaved sedges, sea holly, lamb's ear, Dusty Miller, lungwort (*Pulmonaria*), blue-leaved hostas like 'Abiqua Drinking Gourd', or snow-in-summer (*Cerastium tomentosum*).

Determining Site and Size

Consider planting a white-themed garden near an entryway, along a path leading to a door, surrounding a gate, in a foundation planting, around a deck or patio, or simply in a few pots that flank a walkway, bench, or entry. In a very large garden filled with colorful perennials and annuals, a small area dedicated to white flowers and silver foliage can be a relaxing oasis. If that's the case, site the garden where you enjoy spending time outdoors in the evening. And, since we don't spend every waking hour in our gardens, think about siting it where you can enjoy it from indoors as well.

When developing residential outdoor spaces, great landscape designers consider the view, called sight lines (or site lines), from indoors. Sight lines into the garden are important. Placed in line with a window—whether it's the living room, kitchen, bedroom, or off a patio or deck—a small ornamental tree, a bird bath, an obelisk, a sundial, or a hardscape feature like an arbor, pergola, or a gate adds an interesting focal point that you can always enjoy from indoors, any time of year.

The delicate flowers of blue fescue provide a vertical focal point in the white garden.

Impatiens have long been a cornerstone of many shade gardens.

Start your white garden project with carefully chosen flowers that highlight simplicity and elegance. This approach helps you establish a peaceful corner in your garden, letting you enjoy the soothing atmosphere a white garden provides.

A tree peony's flowers are like delicate crepe paper.

Perhaps you like to sit and relax on a deck at night. A white-flowered moon vine scrambling up the railings and twirling its blossoms open at dusk creates a celestial experience. Or if you entertain outdoors, planting a ribbon of fantastic foliage and fabulous flowers around a patio or deck perimeter will delight your guests. The white garden offers a hint of mystery at dusk and beyond. A few large candles placed on the ground or on a table adds to the evening ambiance.

Before buying plants or seeds, consider how much sun your white garden will receive. Most flowering plants require six hours of direct sunlight. If the planting bed receives less than five hours of sun, consider shade-loving plants such as variegated *Hosta* and *Liriope*, lungwort, white-flowered impatiens, bush anemone (*Carpenteria californica*), and 'Autumn Bride' coral bells (*Heuchera villosa* 'Autumn Bride') among others.

How Large Will It Be?

If you're new to gardening, keep things simple so you won't be overwhelmed. Start with a small area like a 10-foot by 3-foot border. (A border runs along a wall, a fence, a patio, foundation, or deck. A bed is a stand-alone planting area that is often surrounded by lawn, pavers, or other hardscape.)

White gardens are typically intimate spaces. Set the rest of your property apart by planting a small garden with white, silver, gray, and variegated foliage—fascinating and unusual. Select an area where you will enjoy the white flowers at night. Plants flanking an entryway could include flowering vines, such as *Clematis montana* with its large white blossoms, or fragrant yellow jessamine vine (*Gelsemium sempervirens*), native to the southeastern United States. White flowers used near a front entrance or along a driveway will welcome you and your guests on moonlit summer nights. You could also select a spot near a patio, porch, or deck where you can enjoy the garden on a summer evening while you relax or entertain.

The delicate pinkish-white flowers of Portland rose at dusk.

The wonderfully fragrant tobacco flower (*Nicotiana sylvestris*).

A Dreamy Garden

In the ideal garden, there'd be an ever-changing palette of plants coming in and out of bloom. In colder climates, the gardening year begins in spring with snowdrops, daffodils, hyacinths, tulips, pansies, bloodroot, trillium, and other native wildflowers. As the season progresses, the warm-weather-loving annuals and perennials appear on stage. In our garden, white bearded irises, pansies, white alliums, spring snowflake and peonies generally bloom together in mid-spring. Next come perennial daisies, Astilbe 'Bridal Veil', and Siberian irises, as well as a host of annuals— petunias, angel's trumpet, 'Diamond Frost' euphorbia, sweet alyssum, vinca, silver-leaved Dusty Miller, Asiatic lilies and compact Profusion zinnias. In late summer, 'Snowbank' boltonia, hydrangeas, woodland asters, hardy mums and Seven-Son Flower (*Heptacodium*) continue the show until frost arrives. Grouping many plants that like similar growing conditions, in a bed or border, continues the white garden display for many months.

Focus on Fragrance

A key component of the white garden is scent. On warm summer days, many fragrant flowers fill the air from

Hoverflies, bees, and other pollinators visit the flowers of white rugosa rose.

Some flowers like this morning glory have "nectar guides" that are thought to help direct insects to pollen.

you can experience almond and vanilla scents wafting overhead, enhancing the evening's enchantment.

Night Bloomers

Tobacco flower (*Nicotiana sylvestris*) produces densely packed heads of nodding, slim white trumpets that open slightly as they begin releasing their sweet scent at dusk, closing the next morning. Plants that bloom in the evening have evolved to attract night-visiting pollinators like moths and beetles. They have large flowers, generally white and very scented so they are easy to find in the dark. The sweet fragrance often isn't apparent until dusk or later.

Other examples of evening-scented plants include night-blooming jasmine, night-blooming cereus, moonflower vine, night gladiolus (*Gladiolus tristis*), datura, and evening stock (*Matthiola longipetala*), also known as night-scented stock. Place them near seating areas so you can get the full effect of their fragrance and the night-flying pollinators.

Once they are pollinated, the flowers may change color or simply droop, letting pollinators know the pollen is gone. For example, the white flowers of horse chestnut trees have yellow spots before pollination. Once the insects pollinate the flower, the yellow spots turn pink-red, and the bees skip those blossoms.

spring through fall. For example, the season may start with 'Moonlight Sensation' daffodils and white hyacinths followed by white heliotrope, lilies, butterfly bush, lilacs, tuberose, Koreanspice viburnum, sweet alyssum, sweet autumn clematis, and heirloom white roses like 'Blanc Double de Coubert'. Another white heirloom rose, *Rosa alba*, is the emblem of the House of York, represented in England's War of the Roses. On a warm summer night,

The globe-shaped allium flowers appear to float over a bed of sea kale (*Crambe maritima*) while irises are ready to unfurl their blossoms.

Selecting Plants

As you read on, you'll discover bulbs, annuals, perennials, vines, and shrubs for the white garden. Before you buy any plants, check in your region to be sure they are not listed as an invasive species. Invasive plants can overrun native plants and cause problems. Some plants listed in this book may be fine in most areas, but butterfly bush (*Buddleia*), for example, is considered aggressive or invasive in others. See: https://www.invasivespeciesinfo.gov for help when making your selections.

Aim for a long-flowering period by combining bulbs, like this Asiatic lily, with annuals and perennials.

Containers and Window Boxes

Containers

Plant pots and window boxes are among the easiest garden elements to maintain. Once they're planted, all you need to do is water regularly and fertilize once or twice a month during your growing season. Get the most out of your containers by investing in large pots with drainage holes. If there's no way for water to drain out, the potting mix can become waterlogged when it rains, causing the roots to rot. The soil in containers that are less than two feet wide and two feet tall can dry out very quickly in hot weather, which can stress plant roots.

Use a soilless potting mix that contains granular fertilizer. You can find bags at local garden centers and big-box stores. Soilless mixes are lightweight, and unlike heavy garden soil, they tend to drain very quickly. If you find your containers are drying out too quickly (and who really wants to water twice a day), add a layer of compost on top of the soilless mix and this will help retain moisture. Soilless potting mixes can be reused year after year as long as you add some granular fertilizer when replanting, because the nutrients would be depleted after a growing season.

Consider your local weather. If you choose a ceramic pot but live in an area where the temperature dips below freezing, you'll want to empty the container and store it off the ground in a garage or shed so it doesn't crack.

A simple moon garden in a classic urn with caladium as a focal point and bacopa, sedum, ivy and impatiens as fillers and trailers.

A window box planted with twinspur (*Diascia*) greets visitors at the front door.

Use a water-soluble fertilizer once or twice a month during the growing season. There are several products available, such as Bloom Booster and Bloom Plus. Look for one that has "10-54-10" on the label. The numbers stand for Nitrogen-Phosphorous-Potassium. The high middle number for phosphorous indicates that the fertilizer promotes flowering. Follow the instructions for use; adding more fertilizer is not recommended. It's like taking too many vitamins. Just use the recommended amount to maintain healthy plants.

Maintenance

Consider how much time you'll have to maintain the garden. Once it's planted, a border that's 10 feet long and 3 feet wide will need about 20 to 30 minutes a week of maintenance—watering, dead-heading (removing spent flowers), fertilizing, weeding, and checking for insects. In the spring, you'll likely spend more time cleaning the border—cutting and removing dried stems, weeding, dividing perennials that have outgrown their space, amending the soil, adding new perennials or annuals, and covering the soil with a layer of compost. In other words, don't bite off more than you can chew. Start small and make it exquisite.

Star magnolia blossoms emerge in spring to salute the white garden.

What's in a Name?

There are certain words in a plant's name that indicate white, such as alba, album, or albus. Here are the meanings for a few more:

- **ALBIFLORA**: with white flowers
- **ALBOMARGINATA**: white-edged
- **ARGENTEUS**: silvery white
- **CANDICANS**: whitish
- **CANDIDUM**: bright white
- **DEALBATA**: white
- **LACTIFLORA**: with milk-white flowers
- **LEUCANTHEMUM**: with white flowers

Chapter 3

The Elements of Design

"It is the knitting together of so many distinct individuals into a harmonious whole greater than the sum of its parts that makes a garden a garden."

—Elements of Design by Joe Eck (1996)

This patio provides ample space for the table, chairs and the flow of people .

Who doesn't love an outdoor party during summer? A well-designed white garden can be the perfect space to host a celebration, whether it's a wedding, a family reunion, a graduation, or a casual get-together with friends and neighbors.

A garden should feel comfortable and be safe to use not only during the day, but at night since many gatherings continue after dusk. That's where thoughtfully placed lighting around steps, changes in grade, doorways and paths is essential. A fireplace or a firepit surrounded by a white garden keeps the mood going long after sunset.

Outdoor spaces have similar characteristics to those indoors—think about your living room, family room or kitchen. Landscape architects think about those spaces and translate them into outdoor rooms when they are designing gardens. They think of the space as a sequence of steps where homeowners and their guests travel from one spot to the next, just as you move from one room to another in your house.

This large patio serves as an outdoor dining room with an adjacent seating area.

Good planning results in spacious, comfortable seating arrangements. The plants lining the patio are a great example of an understated, white container garden.

A larger patio offers intimate spaces as well as a place to dine.

Over the years, many home builders tended to plunk a small concrete slab behind a house for the patio. It's typically just large enough to hold a table, chairs, and maybe a small grill. Often, guests spill over onto the lawn because the space is too small to hold everyone.

If you're like many homeowners, the patio, deck, or terrace holds a table, chairs, and an umbrella. That arrangement serves a small family for casual meals or relaxing, but for big gatherings, the space should feel roomy as well as functional. The overall size of the patio or deck is generally determined by the number of people who will use the space. Take into consideration the size of the furniture, such as tables, chairs, chaise lounges, as well as a portable or permanent grill, an outdoor kitchen, firepit, or fountain. All these elements make up the garden's entertaining space. The larger, the better. I don't know any homeowner whoever said, "I wish I'd made this smaller." It's usually the other way around.

For sitting or standing on a deck, patio, or terrace, there are functional size requirements that dictate comfort. A rule of thumb tells us that a person standing on a

A pergola and a few drapes cast welcome shade from the setting sun.

patio needs about five square feet of space, while people standing in conversation need about eight square feet per person to feel comfortable rather than cramped.

For a small, round patio table and four chairs, you need a 10-foot by 10-foot space or larger. The "walkaround" space is also important. For comfort, an extra two or three feet of hard surface around furniture allows people to stay on the patio rather than stepping onto the lawn or into planting beds. Just like indoors, in a living room or family room, you want to be comfortable sitting down without constantly moving to let others pass. It's the same with an outdoor living space.

Hot Commodities

There's a trend in patio design—people want fire. Maybe it's a throwback to our human ancestors. A white garden placed around a fire bowl, fire tables, firepit or fireplace adds an exciting element to evenings spent outdoors. Fire features extend the time we spend outside, even on cool days—whether it's early spring or well into fall. Years ago, a campfire ring was the destination in the backyard. A masonry firepit was sometimes placed in a large patio. That has changed with new materials, sleek metal fire tables and gas burners.

The demand for fire elements has become a staple for many patio projects. If you decide to add a fire feature, check your local zoning department for necessary permits and regulations. Zoning requirements often state the minimum distance between the fire feature and structures.

Some municipalities only allow gas rather than woodburning fire features. You might need a plumber to install a gas line. Despite the expense, gas offers convenience because it's easy to start and stop a gas unit rather than adding wood or waiting for a wood fire to extinguish itself.

Fire Tables

Fire tables give that edgy vibe to a new, stylish landscape. They can be the size of a coffee table or as large as a dining room table. A large fire table can be used for dinners, sharing stories, playing cards and board games, or just relaxing and watching the flickering light. They're typically sleek and contemporary and made from fiber-reinforced concrete, aggregates, metals, and other materials. Most are fueled by a propane tank.

A fire table is a contemporary feature for decks, rooftops, and small urban gardens. They are lighter than natural stone, and because they generally are not a permanent structure, you can take it with if you move.

A fire table and comfy chairs face a border filled with white-flowered astilbe. (Designed by Rosborough Partners.)

Pull up a comfortable seat and enjoy the flickering flames at night.

A well-designed and professionally installed fireplace adds value to a home.(Both designs by Hursthouse, Inc.)

The rectangular shapes are very popular. Fire tables are available at big box stores and online, as well as from landscape contractors. But you should shop around and look at reviews.

Firepits

The main difference between a firepit and fireplace is how you want to use it. A firepit is reminiscent of a council ring where family and friends can gather around the fire and share stories across it. The fireplace is something you sit in front of. Stories can still be told but the structure is the focal point and you typically sit facing it. Some firepits are lit by a match and others have a remote button to start.

Some gas-fueled firepits have ceramic logs. And there are portable wood-burning firepits that can be moved around. Check with your municipality about the maximum size allowed for a firepit and how far away it must be from the house and any other building on the property.

An Outdoor Fireplace

A fireplace can be a wonderful feature in the garden. Hiring a landscape contractor rather than attempting a do-it-yourself project can save money and headaches. The chimney must be built so that it's long-lasting and drafts properly. Among all fire features, fireplaces are generally the most expensive. They require a concrete foundation for support and an adequate size chimney to achieve the right draft so smoke doesn't blow back into the patio. Before adding any fire feature, check with your local municipality about regulations and permits.

Water Features

A garden is an invitation to a wonderful sensory experience. Flowers are the eye candy. Roses and herbs offer fragrance for the nose. There's the rustling of leaves with the wind and the sound of birds singing in the morning and at dusk. These elements make a garden inviting, but a water feature adds a whole new dimension. Water reflects the color of the sky and the patterns of the clouds. It can provide delicate trickling, cascading, and bubbling tones—or it might add a whimsical spouting effect. Water attracts wildlife, such as dragonflies (they don't bite) and songbirds looking for a place to bathe or drink, especially in hot or dry weather. Water is often an overlooked feature for residential gardens, but the sound of bubbling water can be very relaxing. It can also mask some of the street noise in urban areas.

An ornamental water feature can be as simple as a fountain, a birdbath, or a contemporary pondless waterfall. It can be a deep, koi-filled pond, where water cascades gently over large boulders and flows slowly down a meandering stream. Whatever form it takes, water adds tranquility, provides pleasant reflections of the sky, and adds ambiance, especially at night.

A spout of water, subtle lighting, and the creamy white flowers of panicle hydrangea create an elegant place to relax at night. (Designed by Hursthouse, Inc.)

A bubbling fountain lit at night adds drama to the garden and can be enjoyed here from indoors or outside. (Designed by Hursthouse, Inc.)

An easy way to bring water into the garden is with a pondless water feature. It can be a slab of beautiful, textured stone with a sheet of water that flows gently over the top and into a basin before it recirculates. It can be a stone or glass sphere from which water bubbles out of the top and flows down the sides. This type of water feature has a contemporary feel and it can be placed in a white garden in a courtyard, near a front entrance or on a patio. Not only do pondless water features require very little maintenance, but they also attract songbirds in search of a drink or a bath.

A self-contained waterfall or "mini" stream provides the beauty and the calming sounds of water without all the maintenance and expense of a pond. These features use a recirculating system that pumps water from an in-ground reservoir through a spillway, over rocks and back into the reservoir.

With its soft splash of water, a fountain provides soothing sounds that transform the space into a peaceful retreat. A fountain can be as simple as a large ceramic pot with a bubbler pump that gently stirs the water. A bonus—moving water is a deterrent to mosquitoes.

Water is one of life's vital elements, so it's no surprise that we find ourselves attracted to it. A water feature can be as simple or as elaborate as you desire. It can also be educational for children. Because water attracts different types of birds and interesting insects like delicate, but harmless, damselflies and dragonflies, children can learn to appreciate nature by observing these beneficial visitors. Time spent near a backyard "stream" or any other water source has a calming effect. What better place to enjoy water but in your own garden?

A waterfall and a woodburning firepit dazzle day and night.

A pondless waterfall fits into a small garden and requires less maintenance than a large-scale pond.

The gentle sound of trickling water helps block out urban noise.

The drama of this fountain made from a Louisiana sugar bowl is amplified with night lighting. (Designed by Hursthouse, Inc.)

Trellises, Obelisks, Arbors, and Pergolas

There's much to be said about the importance of garden structures, such as paths, patios, arbors, trellises, pergolas, and decks. Structure, or hardscape, serves as the groundwork before we begin adding the eye candy—in this case, white flowers and silver-gray foliage. But most any gardener can relate to this: you get to the garden center in spring and go gaga over all the stuff that's in bloom. You load up the car with a floral fantasy of pots, perhaps without giving much thought about what will go where or with what. It's easy to get swept away with flowering plants and that's fine. Flowers, with all their exuberance are likely one of the main reasons you were attracted to gardening in the first place. But there's great value to adding hardscape to your property. Here are some of the structures to consider.

Trellises

Placed against a house, a garage, a fence or set free-standing in a border, trellises provide a vertical element

that is often overlooked. Some gardeners want a trellis for growing vines or climbing roses, others want it to screen views or delineate space. A trellis can be a versatile workhorse in almost any landscape.

A decorative trellis and arbor create an inviting walkway into the back garden.

There's often a design opportunity to use at least one trellis to take advantage of space and to grow plants upward in a narrow border. One or more large trellis panels can be used to create "walls" in an outdoor room and provide privacy without creating a claustrophobic feeling. A trellis panel can screen a less-than-desirable view by distracting the eye, rather than blocking the view. And, trellises, unlike solid fences, are neighbor-friendly.

Sometimes a structure is simply the best solution for the space, depending upon the situation. Other times, it's the extra design element that sets your garden apart from the rest. The choice of materials, size and the amount of detail will affect the cost.

Trellises are made from pressure-treated lumber, western red cedar, fir, rustic wood, aluminum, Corten weathering

A small trellis is perfect for scrambling vines.

A decorative trellis can complement a home's architecture.

steel, and resin. You can buy inexpensive ones at big box stores or have one custom made. Pick a material and color that enhances the style of your home.

The best trellises are those that take cues from the architecture. For example, if you have window muntins (strips of metal or wood that hold the glass panes in place) are they rectangular or square? Is there a rectangular or arched transom window over the entryway? Those shapes will give you cues on how to choose a trellis that complements your house.

Arbors and Pergolas

An arbor acts like a doorway leading into a garden room. It can be used to separate one area from another or it can be an inviting entry point into a side yard. A pergola is simply an extended arbor

Custom-made freestanding trellis panels offer privacy without entirely blocking the view. (Designed by Keith Allen Garden Structures.)

A pergola creates a hallway to the back garden.

and acts more like a hallway or a ceiling over a patio or deck. Arbors and pergolas offer a place to grow flowering vines, which adds a nice element to the white garden.

An arbor or pergola also can serve as a focal point that's viewed from indoors. A pergola covering a patio or deck creates some shade, or it can be set away from the house. Like trellises, arbors and pergolas can be found in materials like cedar, fir, other woods, metal, and resin. Choose an option that complements the style of your house and that is constructed from long-lasting material.

Obelisks and Tuteurs

Obelisks and tuteurs are vertical elements for flowering vines. They can also serve as a piece of art, simply set in a border as a focal point. Like trellises, they make use of vertical space in a small garden. They are decorative elements made from wood, metal, or resin. Some rustic-type tuteurs are made from branches and twigs. Obelisks have a variety of shapes and sizes, but the typical shape is a four-sided, tall and rounded upright form. Tuteurs tend to be three-sided like a pyramid, wider at the base than at the top. In the white garden, either one could support a climbing rose, a moonflower vine, clematis, or white-flowered morning glories.

A rustic obelisk made from twigs.

Two 10-foot obelisks set off drifts of white and silver annuals at Rotary Botanical Gardens in Janesville, Wisconsin.

Painted a flat black, this formal tuteur serves as a piece of art in Frank Mariani's garden in Lake Forest, Illinois.

Lighting

Soft, ambient lighting gently illuminates the facade of the house, accentuating its architectural details and creating a warm, inviting atmosphere.

A garden should feel comfortable and be safe, particularly at night, since you'll be spending time outdoors after dusk. That's where thoughtfully placed lighting around steps, changes in grade, doorways and paths is essential. Night lighting is particularly nice in entertaining areas, like a deck or patio, as well as around the perimeter of the garden. Unlike those bright floodlights positioned over the garage door in the name of security, there are many subtle ways to light and enhance your garden. A lighted landscape is a way of extending the house outside. It's also a creative way to enhance your white garden.

Check with your municipality to see if permits are needed for installation or if a licensed electrician is required to do the work. A professional lighting designer can do much to create a look that's dramatic and appropriate to the size and style of the house, using special techniques such as rope lighting for gazebos, arbors, handrails, or banisters.

Unlike indoors where it's always dry, outdoor lights are subjected to various weather—extreme heat and/or freezing temperatures, snow, hail, rain and perhaps kids, dogs, and sprinklers. These are all things to consider when choosing lights.

Feature Lighting

A light suspended in the canopy of a large shade tree casts a web of delicate shadows, simulating moonlight. And when lighted from below, a crab apple, Japanese maple, redbud, or other small ornamental tree creates a dramatic display. Lighting the steps or walkway to the door is also practical and welcoming. Don't overlook using lanterns with candles or tiki torches. Placed around a patio, they create a warm glow in the evening, and they'll make your white flowers come alive.

Lighting your garden and patio need not be an expensive endeavor. With a few solar lights and some overhead string lights, you can easily add a cozy feel.

Lighting Tips

Consider what you see from indoors and from the street. Could lighting enhance the view of objects or plants? Is there a small ornamental tree, an arbor, fountain, or some other focal point that would benefit from uplighting or a large, mature tree that could use downlighting? Could the path to the driveway be lighted for safety?

Look at architectural elements on your house—decorative siding or beams, for example—that could benefit from lighting. Consider emphasizing structures and plantings by mounting low-voltage halogen bulbs in the eaves of a gazebo or at the base of an arbor. You may want to work with a lighting designer who is familiar with local codes, electrical loads, plant material, low- and high-voltage systems and, most important, someone who is sensitive to your needs, desires, and budget. Ask to see examples of their work and look at customer reviews. Lastly, avoid unshielded bright lights shining into your neighbor's property. And don't over-light your property or it will look like an airport.

Umbrella lights infuse the space with a lively ambiance, setting the perfect mood for an evening gathering.(Design by Hursthouse, Inc.)

Lighting Techniques

These definitions explain the variety of lighting techniques that add drama to your landscape and home.

Downlighting: Lighting an object or surface from above with a large floodlight or several smaller lights.

Moonlighting: Light source is positioned high above the ground and simulates a diffused light. Often used to cast a soft, natural light from treetops.

Uplighting: Lighting an object from below. It can be subtle, creating a silhouette as it captures autumn leaves or swirling snow.

Area lighting: Uniform and bright, this ambient, subtle lighting, often placed over a deck or patio, provides enough light to entertain.

Safety lighting: Lights used on pathways that allow you to move safely through the landscape without stumbling. May include low path lights or stair lights.

Security lighting: Lights used to illuminate and eliminate shadows on entryways, such as doorways, garage doors, steps and pathways.

Grazing: The light is positioned to highlight a surface texture—a brick wall, fence, door, tree trunk, etc.

Spotlight: An intense beam of light that discreetly highlights an important element, such as an entryway, arbor, statue or other focal point.

Accent light: Small spotlight used to highlight a plant or small garden element, such as a fountain, birdbath, obelisk or architectural feature.

Silhouette: A concealed light source, placed in the ground or behind an object, such as a statue, fountain or unusual plant, to create a dramatic silhouette. Especially effective if the light is reflected on a wall or other vertical surface behind the object.

Shadow lighting: Similar to silhouetting, this type of light is used to create a shadow effect on a wall or fence. Particularly effective when it casts the shadows of tree limbs or trelliswork onto a nearby surface.

A small, decorative pond with subtle lighting can provide a soothing place to relax at night.

Contour lighting: Lights used to define perimeters on elements such as driveways or garden beds. Used away from the house, contour lighting gives perspective to the garden.

Mirror lighting: Lights used around the perimeter of a garden pool to capture nearby elements, such as trees, which are reflected in the water.

Cross light: Lighting an object from two or more angles.

Chapter 4

Siting the White Garden: Sun, Shade, and Soil

When you decide where to plant your white garden, you'll need to take note of how much light the area receives and what the soil is like. First, the terms "shade" and "sun" have many definitions that can mystify a new gardener. Take your pick: full sun, part sun, part shade, light shade, dense shade, dry shade, moist/wet shade, heavy shade, high shade, dappled shade, moderate shade, and morning versus afternoon shade or sun. It's enough to confuse any gardener because "sunny" and "shady" are open to interpretation. Understanding how much sunlight reaches areas of your garden is key to selecting plants that will thrive.

Sunlight in spring and fall is less intense because the sun is at a lower angle in the sky. By the summer solstice—around June 21—the sun is at its highest point overhead and is at its brightest. On a cloudless day, sunlight is most intense between 10 a.m. and 3 p.m. When you're in the garden, note where the sun, shade, and shadows occur during those hours.

The amount of direct summer sunlight your garden receives impacts your plant choices. Plants need sunlight to make their own food via a process called photosynthesis. Plants convert sunlight and carbon dioxide from the air and water into oxygen and organic compounds. Different plants require different levels of sunlight to produce enough food for growth, flowering, health, and overall vigor. You'll want to match a plant's light requirements to its location in your garden.

Choosing plants based on their light requirements will lead to success.

Sunlight is at its most intense at the summer solstice in June.

How Much Light and When?

Shade varies in intensity. Many shade-tolerant plants can also handle quite a bit of sun. Often, it's the time of day when they are exposed to sunlight that makes a big difference. For instance, morning sun is less intense. On the east-facing side of our house, I planted tree peonies, sedges, and ferns that benefit from the morning sun, but are protected from afternoon rays and intense summer

Foliage becomes more important than flowers in the white shade garden.

heat. Many shade plants, like hosta, hellebore, Japanese forest grass (*Hakonechloa*) and barrenwort (*Epimedium*) are perfectly content with morning sun alone. Plant them where they'll be exposed to midday sun, and they'll bear the full brunt of solar heat and light. This kind of sun exposure will often burn the leaves of shade-tolerant plants.

Embrace the Shade

Shade won't prevent you from creating a lovely white garden. While plants like petunias and roses won't thrive in a shady site, there are some sun-loving plants, like daylilies, that will grow in light or partial shade. In an area that receives no direct sunlight (such as the north side of a building), many plants will prosper if there is bright or reflected light and if the plants are carefully chosen to fit that environment. Some sun-loving plants, such as bee balm (*Monarda*) and coneflowers, may grow in a shady site if there is dappled or direct sunlight for a few hours during the morning or afternoon. Keep in mind that they'll produce fewer flowers.

Annual vinca (*Catharanthus roseus*) is a sun-loving plant that will grow in light shade but with fewer flowers.

Siting the White Garden: Sun, Shade, and Soil 69

Shade provides a gardener with many opportunities. Consider substituting foliage for flowers. Select plants with leaves of various sizes, shapes, and textures. White flowers and foliage that's variegated—green and white leaves—are particularly lovely in a shade garden, especially on hot summer days. There are many varieties of hostas and lungwort (*Pulmonaria*) with variegated leaves, as well as fragrant tropical plants such as tuberose and jasmine that can be used in pots as focal points in a shade garden.

Basic Definitions

Full sun means that a plant receives a minimum of six hours or more of direct sun each day during the growing season. This could be from 8 a.m. to 2 p.m., 10 a.m. to 4 p.m., etc., as long as it is direct sunlight. It need not be continuous sunlight—it could be four hours in the morning with shade at midday, and two to four hours of sun again in the afternoon.

Calamint is a long-blooming perennial that thrives in full sun.

Light shade is sunlight filtered through a tree that has small leaves or a more open canopy (like a river birch or honey locust). A sugar maple or an oak tree with a dense canopy of leaves will cast more shade.

In shaded areas, the interplay of leaf textures and colors becomes paramount, as it compensates for the lack of bright sunlight, ensuring the garden retains depth, vibrancy, and visual appeal.

Partial shade (or partial sun) refers to sun for part of the day—a few hours in the morning, at midday, or in the afternoon. This is generally between four and five hours of sun a day. It could be dappled sunlight coming through a tree canopy, for example.

Full shade means that a plant receives no direct sunlight. Examples include areas beneath densely branched evergreens, under trees with dense canopies (such as sugar maples), in the shadow of a tall building, under a deep overhang, or at the base of a north-facing wall or fence. Plants that require sun may have lush growth in shade, but very few flowers. And some sun-loving plants will decline or disappear without the light they need.

To some degree, shade can be modified by having an arborist limb up the tree (remove branches) to allow more sunlight to reach the ground. Though many plants are flexible about their cultural requirements, there are limits. You won't have success with roses if your garden is in full or part shade all day. But even with full shade, you can create rich and varied effects with plants having colored or variegated foliage and with white-flowering, shade-tolerant annuals and perennials.

Soil and Site Considerations

Every garden site offers its own unique combination of soil types and drainage. You may well discover that some of your plants thrive in very different conditions than those listed on the plant tag. (The plants obviously haven't read the books, the tags or seed catalogs.) Plant problems can often be the result of poor soil—compacted and hard, too sandy, lacking nutrients or too wet.

Adding organic matter will improve sandy or clay soils.

Leaves may become chlorotic (yellowed) when a plant can't get the nutrients it needs.

Know Your Dirt

Soil is the "living" layer of the earth. It's typically a mix of decomposed rocks (minerals), plants and animals, and microorganisms (bacteria and fungi) too tiny to see without a powerful microscope. The space between the particles holds air and water. The particles that make up soil range from the largest (sand and gravel) to the tiniest (clay).

In sandy soils, the particles and spaces are large, and the water tends to run through quickly. The water may move so fast that the plants are not hydrated properly. In clay soils, the particles are extremely small. When the soil is wet the particles stick together, becoming rock hard once it dries. In water-logged soils, the roots are deprived of needed oxygen. Healthy soil offers moisture and organic material and nutrients that plants need for growth and vigor.

Fixing the Soil

When we step on planting beds or use heavy machinery, the weight compresses the soil particles, pushing out needed spaces for air and water. The soil may become so hard that the water can't reach the roots and they may have a difficult time growing. In areas with heavy clay soil, it's not unusual to pick up a clump after a rain and roll it between the hands where it forms a cigar shape! In an ideal situation, moist clay soil that has been amended with compost will be moist but crumbly.

The best soil is loose, crumbly, and rich with organic matter. If your garden has loam (a mix of sandy silt and clay), you have hit the jackpot (as soil goes). Loamy soil feels spongy and compacts readily into a ball when squeezed but also crumbles. It's easy to work, retains nutrients and water, and does not remain waterlogged.

Adding organic matter regularly helps maintain soil fertility and structure. Examples of organic matter include compost, composted manure, chopped up leaves, and weed-free straw. Dig it into the top three to four inches of soil before planting or in the fall when cleaning up the garden. For containers, use half soilless potting mix and some compost, which increases fertility and water-holding capacity. A top dressing of compost after planting helps suppress weeds and retain moisture.

Sandy Soil

If you have dry soil that's sandy or contains gravel, enrich it with plenty of organic matter such as compost, shredded leaves, or well-rotted manure—whatever is readily available and inexpensive. The addition of organic matter and mulching is important for most soils but is particularly useful for retaining moisture in sandy soils. If you live in an area with water restrictions, try planting a small section of the garden, let the plants become established, then move on to the next area, especially if you have limited time or resources. This will go a long way to giving perennials the start they need to adapt to dry growing conditions. Group plants together with similar water requirements so that watering will be most efficient.

Soil Tests

Do-it-yourself soil test kits.

Just as a blood test determines your health, a soil test determines soil health. The results tell you what's there and what's missing. Soil lacking in certain nutrients can cause yellowing leaves, poor growth, or lack of flowers. Before you douse the plants with fertilizers, which may not be necessary, a soil test can tell you what, if any, fertilizers or amendments are needed.

Garden centers, seed catalogs, and big-box stores offer do-it-yourself soil test kits for homeowner use. If you want a more detailed report, see if your state has a university with a Cooperative Extension Service. The Cooperative Extension Service can direct you to local soil or agricultural laboratory test sites. Or search the internet by entering your state's name and "soil test lab."

A soil or agricultural laboratory website will provide details on how to collect and submit the soil sample as well as the cost for different types of tests, including those for heavy metals and toxic materials such as lead, arsenic, mercury and other toxins. In all, a basic soil test is a good place to start before choosing plants for your white garden.

Sweet or Sour Soil

Soil is categorized as "sweet" (alkaline) or "sour" (acid). It is measured by a pH scale ranging from 1 to 14. The symbol pH is used to express a level of acidity or alkalinity. A pH reading of 7.0 is considered neutral, readings below 7.0 are acidic, and readings above 7.0 are alkaline. Most garden plants grow satisfactorily in soils with a pH level between 6 and 7.

A pH meter from a garden center will indicate whether your soil is alkaline or acid.

For you non-chemistry majors, the term pH stands for a gauge of hydrogen-ion concentration (potential hydrogen) in a substance. For the gardener, it simply means whether the soil is alkaline or acidic. That's important because some plants need specific nutrients that can only be accessed when the soil pH reading is in a certain range. You can easily determine your soil pH with an inexpensive pH meter or a soil test kit that can be purchased at big-box stores, garden centers, or online. There are many plants that are specific in their pH needs, such as rhododendrons (azaleas) that like an acidic soil, while lilacs and clematis prefer a more alkaline soil. Others, like some big-leaf hydrangeas, will change color depending on the soil pH.

Plants may sometimes exhibit nutritional deficiencies that can be addressed by adjusting the pH with sulfur or lime soil amendments. Adding lime will raise the pH of soil, making it more alkaline. Some gardeners are tempted to fertilize plants at the first sight of yellowing leaves or dropping flowers. However, no amount of fertilizer will improve plant health until the pH is adjusted. In the Chicago area, our soils tend to be highly alkaline because of the underlying limestone base. Adding sulfur will lower the pH of the soil, making it slightly more acidic.

Fertilizing

Fertilizer purchased in garden centers typically contains nitrogen for foliage, phosphorous for root establishment and fruit formation, and potassium for root development and disease resistance. A package of fertilizer typically displays three main ingredients on the label shown as three letters (N-P-K). For example, it may display Nitrogen (N), Phosphoric Acid (P_2O_5) and Potash (K_2O). A package labeled 10-10-10 contains 10 percent nitrogen, 10 percent phosphoric acid

and 10 percent potash. The remaining 70 percent of the product may include minor elements like zinc, boron, or magnesium as well as fillers.

Some fertilizers are water soluble. The powder or crystals are added to water and used on flowering plants once or twice a month during the growing season. Granular fertilizer can be added to soil or container potting mix to replenish lost nutrients. Read the label to determine how much you may need. For example, a 15-pound bag of 10-10-10 granular fertilizer is typically used for 1,000 square feet of garden space. Apply granular fertilizer to

Check the labels on granular and water-soluble fertilizers.

the soil just before planting. Spade, till or rake it into the top 4 to 6 inches of white soil. Don't be tempted to use more fertilizer than what's recommended on the label. Doing so can burn the plant roots.

Water

My rain gauge is a super helpful tool. Many times, we have an inch or so of rain, but some of it bounces off leaves and ends up on the patio, driveway, or sidewalk. When I water with the hose, I may not always be certain about how much water reached the roots. In that case, I use a trowel to dig a few inches next to the plant to see how far down the soil is moist. If you're new to gardening, digging into the soil like that will show you how much or little water reached the bottom roots.

There's no need to water every day unless you are watering container plants and the weather is hot. A good rule of thumb is water deeply but infrequently. When the water soaks deep down, the roots will grow downward. If the water is always on the top inch or two of the soil surface, roots will grow upward in search of the moisture.

Successful gardening depends upon the moisture a particular plant receives. Most plants require soil that is moist, but well-drained. When conditions become

Annabelle hydrangea prefers moist soils, especially when planted in full sun.

Compost bins serve a dual purpose: they transform kitchen and garden waste into valuable soil amendments while reducing the environmental impact of discarding organic matter into landfills.

dry and temperatures rise, plants lose moisture through their leaves. The end result is that a plant may wilt or go dormant. While some plants tolerate less moisture, they will not survive drought. Supplemental watering and a layer of organic mulch will help keep them healthy.

Good growing conditions include plentiful organic matter. Enhance your soil's water-holding capacity by incorporating several inches of leaf mold, compost, or well-rotted manure before planting. For existing plants, spread a shallow layer of mulch, leaf-mold, or compost around the base of the plants, but don't pile it on the crowns or stems. That can cause stem rot and encourage insects and fungal disease.

Very few plants will survive in constantly wet soils because the roots are robbed of oxygen. For those intermittently wet areas, consider using native plants that tolerate wet feet. Red-twig dogwood, smooth hydrangea (*Hydrangea arborescens*), aronia, buttonbush (*Cephalanthus*), and Woods' rose (*Rosa woodsii*) are just a few examples.

Feed the Soil

Every household generates vegetable and paper waste. Placed in a compost bin, these materials will decompose and become a fine amendment you can add to your soil. You can also compost your yard waste (untreated lawn clippings, twigs, leaves, etc.). Besides homemade compost, other examples of organic amendments include composted manure, leaf mold (ground-up leaves), and fish emulsion, which can be purchased at garden centers.

A cubic yard of space is all you need to get a compost pile going. Use a commercial bin or make your own enclosure with boards and chicken wire or recycled pallets. Or just layer the following ingredients in a pile in a sunny corner of your garden: one layer of ground-up leaves and chopped up twigs or shredded paper/cardboard, one layer of untreated grass clippings and disease-free plant material, and one layer of soil. As you repeat the layers, water each one. Turn the pile every two weeks in warm weather so the microorganisms continue to break down the waste. Dark, earthy, crumbling compost will be ready for your garden in four to six months. It's so easy, and it's the best thing you can do for your soil—and your plants. And, you'll be keeping your kitchen and yard waste out of the garbage.

Planting

Root competition from trees should be considered when selecting plants: Some trees, such as maples, can make it difficult for understory plants to get established because shallow, dense tree roots absorb most of the available moisture. There's a frequent gardener's lament, "I can't get grass to grow under my trees, even though I've replanted it over and over." Save your money. The only "grass" that will grow in those conditions is artificial turf. Instead, look to drought-tolerant ground covers, such as sedges, epimediums, hellebores, hostas, native pachysandra, variegated Solomon's seal, native sedum, sweet woodruff, and native woodland wildflowers.

Start off with smaller, drought-tolerant plants that will adapt to these conditions. Trees create mats of fine roots within the top 18 to 24 inches or so of the soil. If too many of these roots are destroyed during soil preparation and planting, the tree may suffer serious damage. When planting under trees, carefully dig individual planting holes and don't use a rototiller. You may wish to start small and phase in the garden under a large tree over a three-year period. When in doubt, select plants in small pots—4 inches or smaller—or buy a flat of plants if you're planting ground covers.

Planting under established trees should be done in phases so the roots are not disturbed.

A Word of Caution

Nature abhors a vacuum. If you weed and leave your soil bare with no mulch or plants, it will soon be filled with seedlings—weeds and trees—that blow into your garden. As in the wild, nature fills the bare soil with seedlings. Consider that when you're laying out your white garden—bare soil is not your friend.

Landscapes change over time. A garden will become more heavily shaded as trees and shrubs mature. As the light changes, shade gardens are usually more subtle, lacking the bright, bold colors and flowering potential found in sunny locations. This is an opportunity to try new types of plants. Take advantage of large-leafed plants, such as hostas or elephant ears to add textural contrast.

Chapter 5

Designing the White Garden

Buying plants is fun. But gardeners are often smitten by all the new and colorful things at garden centers in spring. "Start small and make it exquisite." That was the advice from a long-time gardener many years ago to everyone who visited her one-acre wonderland. If you make your white garden bigger than you can reach across—or have time to maintain, the disappointment is sure to arrive.

Plants need weeding, watering, fertilizing and dead-heading (removing spent flowers). Perennials—plants that return each year—may need lifting, dividing, and replanting every few years. You can always enlarge the garden as you become more familiar with the plants and the amount of time and care your new white garden will need.

The end result begins with a design of your making.

This path in the author's garden showcases how gardening is an art, and all gardeners are artists, combining textures, color, shape, and form.

Much of the pleasure of growing a white garden—or any garden—comes from experimenting with plants. Combining different heights, shapes, textures, and foliage colors is part of being the gardener-artist. Whether you can draw a straight line or not, you are an artist in your garden. I look at our garden as a giant coloring book or living canvas. As gardeners we deal with color, form, and shapes, and like sculpting, we deal with the three-dimensional and with plants that come and go with time. If you garden—even if it's in containers—you are the artist creating something unique.

Plant shopping is fun, but go with a plan and a list.

  White Gardens

Before and after: Initially, the patio deck features colorful plants in rail-top boxes. In the transformation, these are replaced with white blooms, and additional white plants are introduced on the deck, creating a cohesive and refined look.

Before and after: The initial patio border, marked by modest vegetation and bare patches, evolves into a thriving landscape enriched by diverse white plants, elevating the overall ambiance of the walkway.

Designing a White Border

Using vertical plants like this silver-leaved pear alongside rounded, mounding plants adds visual interest.

Whether your white garden will be in sun or shade, you can create visual interest by using plants with contrasting shapes—mounded versus vertical forms, for example. To get the most out of my borders, I like to work in large drifts of plants in odd numbers. For example, if I'm growing white coneflowers, I may use a group of seven or nine to create impact. Because the flowers are round, I use upright plants to create a contrast. If everything was round and mounded, there's nothing to break up your design.

Utilizing drift planting enhances garden impact, creating cohesive, striking displays and a sense of natural flow, highlighting the unique textures of each plant.

Repeating plant shapes throughout the border draws the eye from one end to the other.

Designing a Freestanding Bed

Vertical plants and accents help break up rounded shapes.

Thoughtfully composed, this freestanding white garden bed displays a diverse array of shapes and sizes, featuring tobacco flower, liatris, hisbiscus and daisies.

A freestanding white garden bed is meant to be viewed from all sides—like sailing around an island. When designing an island bed, I usually place the largest and tallest plants in the center and then work my way down to the edges. I also think about the side of the island bed that is in the sight line from the home, deck, or patio.

The amount of sunlight and how it reaches the bed is important. If the back of the bed is mostly in shade, the taller plants may go there, and the rest of the plants can be graduated in height to the front edge. Island beds can be round, square, rectangular, or freeform. Sometimes they are long and narrow depending on the space available. The length and width should be somewhat proportional. At its widest point, if the bed is more than four feet, stepping stones are helpful to avoid compacting the soil when you step into the plantings for maintenance.

Curb Appeal

Whether you live in a ranch, bungalow, Queen Anne, Tudor, Cape Cod, mid-century modern, or another style, the landscape surrounding your home has its own personality, too, especially out front. Perhaps you desire a more formal garden—something that has crisp, straight-edged borders, neatly trimmed shrubs and manicured evergreens, and a rectangular panel of grass. Or perhaps you lean to something more informal, like a cottage garden with billowy, informal borders filled with annuals, perennials, flowering vines, and roses. Both informal and

formal garden designs lend themselves to a white garden. Whatever look you prefer, your front landscape creates a first impression about who lives there and ultimately impacts the resale value of a home.

I've redesigned older gardens that had overgrown evergreens, or shrubs that outgrew their space and were simply tired looking. I've recreated foundation plantings where old yews and junipers were separated and meticulously trimmed into muffins or boxes. Sometime, an older garden simply has too many different plants that don't work together.

If you're thinking about giving your foundation planting a makeover, your goal should be to have it enhance the house and make it look welcoming from the street. Stand on the front sidewalk or cross the street and take a long look at your front landscape to see what plants may be overwhelming the house. Take several photos that you can study later or to show at a local garden center when you're shopping for new plants. Old shrubs can get out of control, become massive, and eat up the adjacent lawn. Consider removing old, overgrown evergreens with plants that are more in scale with the house. Do some of your existing shrubs block the windows or impede the walkway?

Before: an overgrown foundation planting.

After: a renovated foundation planting with an inviting white garden.

You want big plants to frame, not obscure, your house. Old, tired foundation planting can be made simpler with bigger masses of plants and fewer types. When you do buy plant replacements, consider their ultimate size in the ground. Small, cute shrubs in pots are like baby raccoons. They eventually get to be quite large and unruly.

For a modern house, such as a mid-century modern ranch or a contemporary, sleek home, you'll want to create bed lines to mimic the house and use more "architectural" plants—vertical grasses, shrubs, or trees, for example. Bed lines (the edges that meet the lawn) should be simple and clean and the beds spacious enough for plants with room for them to grow. Your foundation planting should embrace the seasons—bulbs in spring, flowering shrubs, long-blooming perennials, and annuals so there's something blooming for several months.

Before: tired foundation planting.

After: a lush white garden with varied shapes and plants creates a cohesive and classic look.

Before: a foundation border in need of a makeover.

After: the border has been cleaned up and filled in with thriving white flowers and variegated foliage.

Pots with Panache

We garden on an acre, but I would never be without my containers. Think of containers as accessories for your white garden and outdoor living space. In small areas, they can be grouped together and staged for a sensational display. Because very few perennials bloom for more than a few weeks, I like to place large pots filled with annuals on our patio, by the front door, on paths, and in borders.

When combining several plants in one pot, I pair those that prefer the same type of culture—light shade or full sun, good drainage or frequent watering. The possibilities are endless. On your next visit to the garden center, pick up a pot, some plants and start designing in your cart. Becoming a garden artist was never easier.

There are a few ways to arrange your plants in pots and window boxes. A monopot container filled with white petunias or impatiens can create a very dramatic and contemporary look. Combopot plantings tend to have a thriller, filler and spiller. The thriller plant is typically upright and vertical, like a grass or a canna lily. The filler could be a rounded plant, such as compact zinnias, while the spiller, which trails over the edge of the pot, could be a vine.

This classic planter features a thriller, filler, and spiller—a fern, white-flowered begonias, coral bells, and trailing ivy.

Thriller, spiller, and filler in this white container combo. (Design by Hursthouse, Inc.)

Pots of dwarf white plume grass serve as vertical elements in this container grouping.

Part 2

Selecting the Plants

Once you've decided where to place your white garden or containers, the next step is choosing the plants. The following chapters aim to inspire, helping you decide whether to use shrubs, perennials, annuals and vines, or a combination of them all. It's essential to think about contrasting plant shapes and the benefit of planting in drifts over using different "specimen" plants. When I choose plants, I consider their bloom duration and coordination. Local weather sometimes impacts this, and perfecting the "wow" performance may require adjustments. For me, gardening becomes "painting" with plants, treating my garden as a living canvas.

In Zone 5, our winters are cold and wet, so I typically plant in spring. However, early fall is also suitable, especially for planting spring-blooming bulbs. Those in warmer zones might have the luxury of planting year-round. Ultimately, gardening is about experimentation. It's never truly finished, and that's its charm. Every season offers a new opportunity to experiment with your plant palette, be it in the ground, a container, or a window box. Now, let's explore some plants.

Chapter 6

All About Annuals

A white garden wouldn't be complete without an array of annuals. They provide long-lasting flower power in beds, borders, hanging baskets, pots, and window boxes. Annuals are plants that complete their life cycle in one growing season—they grow, flower profusely, produce seeds, and die. They are unlike perennials, which return each year, regrowing from hardy rootstock below the soil surface. However, annuals not only provide instant interest, but their bloom period also tends to be much longer than that of most perennials, which may only bloom three or four weeks at best.

Most annuals are quite adaptable to general garden conditions. They need good light, sufficient water, and reasonably fertile soil. Most annuals prefer full sun and well-drained (moist, but never soggy) soil. If your garden offers full sun or part sun, you'll find that there are hundreds of annuals from which to choose. If your garden is mostly shade, there are annuals like New Guinea impatiens, browallia, begonias, violas and caladium, as well as native wildflowers.

Annuals vary according to their cold tolerance. Frost-hardy annuals, such as larkspur, stocks, wallflowers, and pansies, can withstand short periods of frost. In mild climates, frost-hardy annuals are planted in the fall for winter and early spring bloom. In cold climates, frost-hardy annuals are planted in spring after all danger of freezing weather has passed. (See USDA Plant Hardiness Zone Map on page 92.)

If your soil is primarily clay, adding compost, well-rotted manure, or other organic amendments and digging them into the top six inches or so will help loosen the soil, breaking up fine clay particles and allowing for tiny pockets where air, water, and nutrients can reach the roots. On the other hand, if your soil is rocky or sandy, adding these amendments helps retain necessary moisture.

Unlike perennials, annuals must be replanted each year. In some cases, you can save the seeds and start them indoors or sow them directly in the soil outdoors to save money. This often works with marigolds, cosmos, zinnias,

Many annuals like *Plectranthus* and 'Silver Mound' artemisia have stunning silver foliage.

This garden uses varying shades of white and silver, paired with many shapes and sizes of plants and structures, to create a dynamic effect.

Starting annuals from seed like these nasturtiums is easy and inexpensive.

nicotiana and larkspur—older, heirloom varieties that are "open-pollinated." Unlike newer cultivars, the seeds of open-pollinated plants produce offspring that are replicas of the parent plants.

Some annuals, like moss rose (*Portulaca*), nasturtiums, cosmos, poppies, and gazania, do better when grown in soil that is "lean" (not fertile). Lean soil contains fewer nutrients than rich soil. Plants that thrive in poor garden soil evolved in environments where the soil is sandy or rocky, and as a rule, they don't require extra nutrients. All in all, annuals could be considered the long-blooming rock stars of the white garden. Here are some adaptable and versatile annuals to consider.

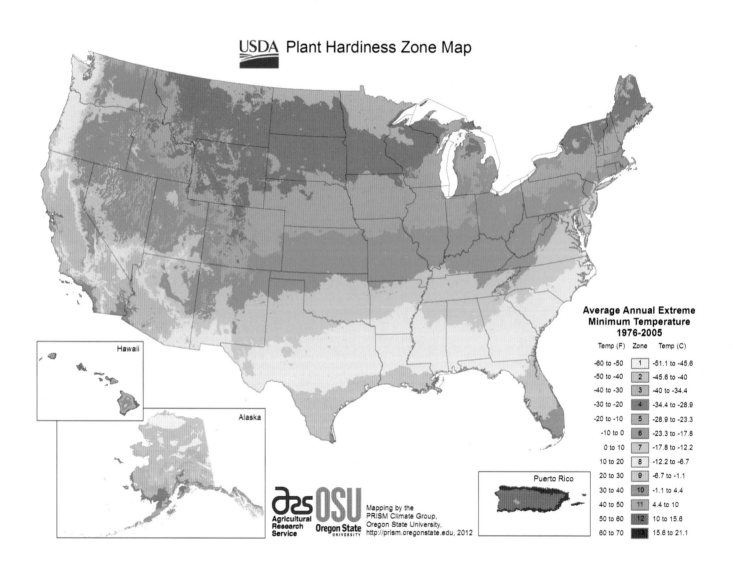

USDA Plant Hardiness Zone Map

Average Annual Extreme Minimum Temperature 1976-2005

Temp (F)	Zone	Temp (C)
-60 to -50	1	-51.1 to -45.6
-50 to -40	2	-45.6 to -40
-40 to -30	3	-40 to -34.4
-30 to -20	4	-34.4 to -28.9
-20 to -10	5	-28.9 to -23.3
-10 to 0	6	-23.3 to -17.8
0 to 10	7	-17.8 to -12.2
10 to 20	8	-12.2 to -6.7
20 to 30	9	-6.7 to -1.1
30 to 40	10	-1.1 to 4.4
40 to 50	11	4.4 to 10
50 to 60	12	10 to 15.6
60 to 70	13	15.6 to 21.1

Hawaii

Alaska

Puerto Rico

Agricultural Research Service

Oregon State UNIVERSITY

Mapping by the PRISM Climate Group, Oregon State University, http://prism.oregonstate.edu, 2012

Sweet Alyssum (*Lobularia maritima*)

Sweet alyssum's dense clusters of tiny white flowers release a honey-scented fragrance on warm summer days and often continue doing that even after the first fall frosts hit northern climates. I like to use this sweet-scented annual in a long-planted ribbon that hugs walkways, our patio, and the front edge of a border. Along our meandering stone path, I sow sweet alyssum seeds in between the limestone slabs to create pockets of evening color and fragrance.

You can also use *Lobularia* to trail over the edge of a pot, window box, or hanging basket. Plants bloom most profusely under cool (60° to 68° F) night temperatures. Seed-grown varieties such as 'Carpet of Snow', typically sold in 4-packs and 6-packs have been around for years, but the plants tend to become leggy in hot weather. The flowering stems elongate and produce many seeds with only a few flowers at the tips. Newer varieties like 'Snow Princess', 'Snow Crystals', and 'White Knight' are among those bred to produce long-blooming, tight compact mounds of flowers that rarely need shearing. They are usually sold in four-inch pots rather than in packs or flats and are more expensive. Sweet alyssum is easy to grow from seed sown outdoors in early spring and again in midsummer for continued bloom.

Sweet alyssum's fragrance along the border's edge lingers after twilight on warm summer nights.

COMMON NAMES: sweet alyssum; **HARDINESS:** cool-season hardy annual that tolerates some light frost; **SIZE:** 6 to 12 inches tall and 18 inches to 2 feet wide, depending on cultivar; **CONDITIONS:** sunny site with well-drained, fertile soil; **CARE:** water when the soil surface feels dry. If flowering slows down in hot weather or plants become leggy, encourage a new flush of growth by cutting stems back a few inches; **PLANT PARTNERS:** Dusty Miller, silver-leaved artemisia, dahlias, cleome, zinnias, roses.

Flowering Tobacco (*Nicotiana sylvestris*)

Impressive stature makes flowering tobacco a fragrant focal point.

Named after Jean Nicot, who introduced tobacco to France in 1560, Nicotiana represents a group of plants that are predominantly easy to grow and thrive in summer's heat and humidity. *Nicotiana sylvestris*, known as woodland tobacco, distinguishes itself in the white garden, providing a striking focal point due to its height, elegance, and fragrance.

Flowering tobacco can thrive in full sun or endure a half day of afternoon shade, the "sylvestris" species typically reaching 5 to 6 feet in narrow, 24-inch spaces. Notable for its star-flaring, tubular flowers, it may self-sow tiny, pepper-sized seeds if it favors its location, adding an unexpected "pop-up" element to gardens. Varieties like *Nicotiana* 'Only the Lonely' and *Nicotiana alata* (jasmine tobacco) emit a distinct, sweet scent during twilight, with the latter standing out for its day-closing blooms. While there are shorter, day-blooming varieties developed, they usually lack the characteristic fragrance.

COMMON NAMES: Flowering tobacco, woodland tobacco, shooting stars; **HARDINESS:** Withstands light frost once established; **SIZE:** 18 inches to 5 feet tall depending on the species or cultivar; **CONDITIONS:** moist, well-drained, humus-rich soil in full sun to light afternoon shade; **CARE:** provide supplemental watering during hot, dry weather; **PLANT PARTNERS:** white-flowered daisies, canna lilies, larkspur, dahlias, marigolds, dill, zinnias, bronze fennel; **NOTE:** use a water-soluble fertilizer every few weeks to encourage blooms.

Devil's Trumpet (*Datura metel*)

Native to China and Southeast Asia, *Datura metel* (or 'Devil's Trumpet') is a vigorous annual that develops pretty blue-green leaves and large trumpet-shaped flowers that face upward. The glistening white trumpets open at twilight and remain open for a 24-hour dazzling show. Flowers are followed by egg-shaped, very prickly seed pods. The plants may sometimes self-sow, showing up in the garden once the soil is warm (in colder climates). In warm regions, the plants are considered tender perennials. *Datura* 'Belle Blanch' reaches 24 to 30 inches tall and wide.

Low-growing angel's trumpet opens at dusk.

COMMON NAMES: Devil's Trumpet, thorn apple, death angel, horn of plenty; **HARDINESS:** does not tolerate frost; tender perennial; prefers warm air and soil; **SIZE:** 24 to 30 inches tall and wide; **CONDITIONS:** well-drained, moist average soil in full sun to light shade; **CARE:** Slow to develop and bloom. Use a water-soluble fertilizer every two weeks to encourage flowering. Water regularly, especially when the weather is hot and dry; **PLANT PARTNERS:** globe amaranth, salvia, Alaska Shasta daisy, snapdragons, ageratum; **NOTE:** All parts are poisonous.

White marigolds add a glow to the evening garden.

COMMON NAMES: marigold; **HARDINESS:** hardy annual; **SIZE:** moonlight marigold is 18 to 24 inches tall and wide; **CONDITIONS:** full sun, well-drained soil; **CARE:** keep young plants evenly moist; **PLANT PARTNERS:** salvia, vinca, penstemon, celosia, sweet alyssum; **NOTES:** remove faded flowers to encourage more blossoms.

Marigold (*Tagetes*)

Marigolds are a large group of annuals called *Tagetes* that are native to subtropical America (and not from Africa or France as some of their common names imply). Marigold flowers are easily recognized by their orange, red, gold, and lemon-yellow flowers. For years, breeders have attempted to create pure white marigold flowers. In 1954, Burpee, a seed company in Warminster, Pennsylvania, launched a contest in hopes of finding a white marigold growing in a home garden. The $10,000 prize for the seeds of a truly white marigold was finally awarded to an Iowa gardener in 1975 and the first-ever white-flowered cultivar, 'Snowbird', was introduced. Others have since followed. *Tagetes erecta* 'Sugar and Spice White' has creamy yellow flowers that fade to a muted white. Moonlight marigold is a bushy carnation-flowered variety that produces masses of very pale-yellow blossoms prefect for sunny beds and borders. The flowers become more abundant in late summer, lighting up the garden at night.

Bishop's Flower (*Ammi majus*)

This Queen Anne's lookalike, *Ammi majus*, deserves a spot in more gardens. The flowers provide a subtle "wow" factor in beds or borders and can be picked when fully open and enjoyed in a graceful arrangement for up to 10 days in a vase. Sow seeds or place transplants in the middle of the border, creating sweeping drifts or using them as fillers among other annuals, perennials, and roses. By midsummer, the slender two-foot-tall branching stems are topped with umbels that look like white lace. Overall, *Ammi majus* is an easy-care, fun annual that attracts pollinators.

COMMON NAMES: Annual Queen Anne's lace, bishop's flower; **HARDINESS:** half-hardy annual; **SIZE:** 3 to 4 feet tall and 1 to 2 feet wide, possibly more; **CONDITIONS:** full sun to part sun, well-drained soil; **CARE:** remove spent blossoms to encourage continued flowering; **PLANT PARTNERS:** hollyhocks, roses, zinnias, sweet alyssum, salvia, penstemon; **NOTES:** Sow seeds directly into the soil. Toxic to pets and horses.

Plant extras so you can use them in cut-flower arrangements.

'Purity White' cosmos.

Cosmos (*Cosmos*)

Cosmos 'Psyche White' produces a flush of ferny foliage topped by 4-inch-wide flowers with yellow centers. Plants reach 3 to 4 feet tall and 2 feet wide. This old-fashioned heirloom is a popular cottage garden plant. It attracts butterflies with its nectar, and goldfinches and other seed-eating birds enjoy the seed heads when the flowers have finished. *Cosmos* 'Purity Sensation' has snow-white flowers that are 4 to 6 inches wide on plants that reach 3 to 5 feet tall.

COMMON NAMES: cosmos; **HARDINESS:** tender annual; **SIZE:** 3 to 5 feet tall depending on cultivar; **CONDITIONS:** full sun, fertile garden soil; **CARE:** use a water-soluble fertilizer once or twice a month during the summer; **PLANT PARTNERS:** zinnias, salvia, petunias, celosia; **NOTES:** flowers make a nice long-lasting addition to a floral arrangement.

Annual white-flowered geraniums offer beefy blooms.

Geranium (*Pelargonium*)

Pelargonium varieties, commonly referred to as geraniums, are adorned with vibrant green leaves and are crowned by clusters of bright flowers that can range from white and pink to deep red. These plants typically grow to about 1 to 2 feet in height with a similar spread. They are a favorite in summer gardens and containers for their continuous blooms and easy care. They attract butterflies with their vibrant colors, and many varieties have uniquely scented leaves that vary from citrus to rose, cherished by gardeners.

COMMON NAMES: geranium; **HARDINESS:** annual; **SIZE:** 12 inches tall and wide or more; **CONDITIONS:** provide a spot with 6-plus hours of sun and fertile, well-drained soil; **CARE:** use a water-soluble fertilizer once or twice a month during summer; **PLANT PARTNERS:** salvia, sweet alyssum, daylilies, Asiatic lilies; **NOTES:** remove spent flowers to encourage more blossoms.

Sunflowers (*Helianthus*)

Most people recognize sunflowers with their gold or yellow ray petals and dark centers. But there are some varieties that offer creamy white blooms. 'Italian White' has smaller, cream-colored flowers than the big 'Russian Mammoth' sunflowers, but what it lacks in size it makes up for in the number of flowers that form on side-branching stems. Plants tend to stay under five feet tall.

COMMON NAMES: sunflower; **HARDINESS:** annual; **SIZE:** 3 to 9 feet depending on cultivar or species; **CONDITIONS:** full sun, dry soil; **CARE:** use a water-soluble fertilizer once or twice a month during summer; **PLANT PARTNERS:** other pale sunflowers, cosmos, nicotiana, daisies; **NOTES:** leave seed heads on the plants to attract seed-eating birds.

'Italian White' sunflowers produce a bounty of 4-inch-wide blossoms.

Caladium (*Caladium*)

Caladiums are wonderful, tropical-looking foliage plants for shade. They are native to Central and Northern parts of South America. They come in multiple combinations of colors, but white and green leaves make the most of white gardens, especially in shady sites. They are grown from tubers that are planted when the soil is warm in spring and when all danger of frost has passed in cold climates. Most *Caladium* cultivars are adaptable to full shade (no direct sunlight), but some tolerate partial sun or early morning dappled sunlight. The tubers can be lifted from the soil and stored in a dry location (in peat moss or shredded paper) at 70° to 75° F until replanting in spring after danger of frost has passed. Some people store the tubers indoors in pots of soil. The plants will lose their leaves over winter and become dormant.

COMMON NAMES: angel wings, elephant's ear; **HARDINESS:** tender annual; **SIZE:** 1 to 2.5 feet tall and wide; **CONDITIONS:** full to part shade, moist, rich soil; **CARE:** provide plenty of organic matter and moist but well-drained soil; **PLANT PARTNERS:** astilbe, impatiens, hostas, begonias, ferns, native woodland wildflowers; **NOTES:** leaves are toxic. Slugs and snails may cause damage.

Attractive caladium leaves brighten a white garden in shade.

Baby's Breath (*Gypsophila elegans*)

This annual *Gypsophila* offers an effect like no other annual. Delicate, tiny flowers continue to bloom from late spring until fall frosts in cold areas. The plants add a frothy touch in between other white-flowered plants in a bed, border, or large container. As a cut flower, the stems offer tiny double flowers on well-branched upright foliage. The plant comes into bloom all at once, producing clouds of flowers that last for many weeks. The plants bloom in about eight weeks from germination, so if you were planning a special event, you could time the bloom. Otherwise, its cousin, *Gypsophila paniculata*, or "florist's baby's breath" tends to be much longer blooming.

COMMON NAMES: annual baby's breath, annual gypsophila; **HARDINESS:** can withstand a light frost; **SIZE:** 12 to 18 inches tall and wide; **CONDITIONS:** full sun and moderately rich, well-drained soil; **CARE:** remove spent flowers to promote blossoming; **PLANT PARTNERS:** zinnias, coneflowers, daisies, roses; **NOTES:** an excellent filler in a border.

A lovely addition to the white garden, baby's breath makes a good cut flower, too.

New Guinea Impatiens
(*Impatiens hawkeri*)

New Guinea Impatiens are vibrant perennials native to the islands of New Guinea. Their white blooms are especially fitting for white gardens in partially shaded areas. Planting begins post-frost in well-draining, consistently moist soil. They thrive in partial shade, protected from harsh afternoon sun, and in cooler climates, they're often grown as annuals, blooming from late spring to early autumn.

COMMON NAMES: impatiens, New Guinea impatiens; **HARDINESS:** tender annual; **SIZE:** 12 inches tall and wide; **CONDITIONS:** part to full shade, morning sun and afternoon shade; fertile soil; **CARE:** use a water-soluble fertilizer once or twice a month during summer; **PLANT PARTNERS:** coleus, *Caladium*, begonias, astilbe, hosta; **NOTES:** add a layer of compost to keep the soil moist.

New Guinea impatiens work well in the ground with other shade-loving perennials or in containers.

Snow-on-the-Mountain
(*Euphorbia marginata*)

Snow-on-the-Mountain is a striking annual known for its green leaves edged with a distinctive white border. Originating from the Great Plains of North America, its unique foliage creates a snowy effect, making it a prime candidate for white gardens. Best sown directly in well-draining soil after the last frost, it thrives in full sun to partial shade. Blooming in late summer, it adds a frosty touch to the landscape through the season.

COMMON NAMES: snow-on-the-mountain; **HARDINESS:** tender annual; **SIZE:** up to 3 feet tall and wide; **CONDITIONS:** full sun and well-drained soil; **PLANT PARTNERS:** ornamental grasses, nicotiana, cleome, dahlias, zinnias; **NOTES:** Avoid getting the sap on bare skin. Save the hard round seeds to sow the following spring.

The flowers are insignificant, but the leaves of *Euphorbia marginata* light up the garden day or night.

White annual salvia provides vertical accents in the border.

Salvias (*Salvia*)

There are many species of *Salvia*, but the annuals, like mealycup sage (*Salvia farinacea*), offer a long season of bloom. With their vertical flowers, they make a nice counterpoint to cosmos and zinnias. Once established, they are drought-tolerant, and they attract bees, butterflies, and hummingbirds. If space allows, use them in large drifts.

COMMON NAMES: mealycup sage; **HARDINESS:** tender annual; **SIZE:** 1½ to 2 feet tall and 16 to 18 inches wide; **CONDITIONS:** full sun to light shade; **PLANT PARTNERS:** cosmos, geraniums; **NOTES:** a good plant for beds, borders and containers.

Zinnia (*Zinnia*)

Few flowers are as redolent of summer as zinnias. The range of colors includes just about every shade except blue. But there are many beautiful white, pale yellow, and chartreuse zinnias that work in a white garden. There's the compact 8-inch-tall 'Crystal White' zinnia with its single, small, daisy-like blooms that cover stems all season. At 16 inches tall 'White Wedding' boasts 4-inch-wide double flowers and there are many others to choose from. Although powdery mildew plagues old-fashioned, taller zinnias, disfiguring the leaves with a blanket of white in late summer, newer varieties like 'Profusion White', and 'Oklahoma White' have low susceptibility to powdery mildew. The latter grows from 30 to 40 inches tall and has prolific 2-inch-wide double and semidouble, pure white flowers. Zinnias are easy to grow from seed or buy a tray of small plants and transplant them into the garden after the last spring frost date if you live in a colder area. All zinnias make great cut flowers for a white garden arrangement.

Zinnias attract pollinators and make great cut flowers.

COMMON NAMES: zinnia, youth-and-old-age; **HARDINESS:** tender annual; **SIZE:** from 6 inches to 40 inches tall depending on the cultivar; **CONDITIONS:** full sun, well-drained, rich soil; **CARE:** remove spent flowers on taller varieties to promote additional blossoms; use granular fertilizer when planting and a water-soluble fertilizer once or twice a month during the growing season; **PLANT PARTNERS:** salvia, milkweeds (*Asclepias*), celosia, dusty miller; **NOTES:** no matter how large or small the blossoms, zinnias look beautiful in a vase.

Chapter 7

All About Perennials

Perennials are those plants that live for many years unless they're affected by disease, cold, humidity, drought, or the wrong growing conditions, such as soil that's too wet or too dry for their liking. Trees and shrubs can be considered perennial plants but most garden perennials are herbaceous—plants with soft, non-woody stems. In colder parts of the country, the top growth (leaves, flowers, and stems) of perennials like coneflowers and ferns will die above ground. In warmer climates, the leaves may still be green until winter. And in very warm, frost-free areas, the same plants may keep their leaves and continue flowering through the winter months.

Perennials are sometimes referred to as hardy or tender. Hardy perennials can survive low winter temperatures. However, some cold-hardy hardy perennials struggle in warm, humid regions. Tender perennials are those that can't survive low temperatures. In Northeastern Illinois, we treat these plants as annuals. One example is mealycup sage (*Salvia farinacea*), which is an annual in my garden, but can survive over winter in some Southern states.

There are hundreds of great perennials for use in sunny and shady gardens. You could do an entire border of perennials, but I like to mix in annuals to continue the bloom throughout the growing season. One word of caution: make sure the plants that you buy are not aggressive spreaders. Although I love gooseneck loosestrife (*Lysimachia clethroides*) for its white arching spikes of small, tightly packed flowers, it took over an entire perennial border. It took many hours to dig out the roots to eradicate it. There are many well-behaved perennials that are lower maintenance. The following are a few favorites. Your local garden centers will have many more.

Milkweed, a versatile perennial, thrives across diverse climates, enhancing gardens with its unique aesthetic and supporting local ecosystems.

Chosen with care, the right perennials can be long-lived plants in the white garden, such as these in the Moonlight Meadow at Olbrich Botanical Gardens in Madison, Wisconsin.

'Ice Ballet' milkweed offers nectar to many pollinators and a place for female monarch butterflies to lay their eggs.

Ice Ballet Milkweed
(*Asclepias incarnata 'Ice Ballet'*)

I love monarch butterflies and plant many nectar-rich flowers for them. But they also need milkweed on which to lay eggs. In fact, they will only lay their eggs on milkweed plants. The common milkweed (*A. syriacus*) is a running plant that would quickly take over our borders, so I use other, well-behaved species like swamp milkweed. 'Ice Ballet' is a swamp milkweed cultivar with white flowers. It attracts many pollinators and female monarch butterflies. And the flowers are lightly fragrant. Although the common name is "swamp" milkweed, plants tolerate rich, well-drained garden soils.

COMMON NAMES: swamp milkweed; **HARDINESS:** zones 3 to 9; **SIZE:** 3 to 4 feet tall and 1½ to 2 feet wide; **CONDITIONS:** full sun and medium to wet soil; **CARE:** plants have deep taproots and are best not moved once planted; **PLANT PARTNERS:** garden phlox, turtlehead (chelone), culver's root; **NOTES:** slow to emerge in spring; keep roots moist until plants are established.

White Blazing Star
(*Liatris spicata* 'Floristan White')

Our native blazing star is a wonderful plant for the sunny garden and although the flowers are typically violet or light purple, there are white-flowered cultivars. In our garden, blazing stars attract butterflies, bees, and hummingbirds! The flowers open slowly from top to bottom over a period of a week or so. I leave the stalks standing for winter interest and for seed-eating birds.

COMMON NAMES: blazing star, gayfeather; HARDINESS: zones 4 to 8; SIZE: 3 feet tall and 1 to 2 feet wide; CONDITIONS: full sun, moist, well-drained soil; CARE: if planting corms in spring, place them just below the soil surface; PLANT PARTNERS: phlox, milkweed, culver's root, annuals; NOTES: emerging plants look like grass in spring so take care when weeding.

Liatris creates a vertical focal point in beds and borders.

False dragonhead is another great vertical plant to play off mounded perennials.

False Dragonhead
(*Physostegia virginiana*)

This native species is nicknamed obedient plant because the flowers can be moved left or right and will temporarily remain in that position. (A fun plant for kids and adults!) In its natural habitat in North America, it grows from Quebec to Manitoba to Florida and New Mexico. There is a pink variety, but it's the white-flowered cultivars—'Crystal Peak White', 'Crown of Snow', and 'Alba'—that I like for the white garden. Flowers start to bloom from bottom to the top of each spike. A bonus: these plants attract hummingbirds!

COMMON NAMES: false dragonhead, obedient plant; HARDINESS: zones 3 to 9; SIZE: 3 to 4 feet tall and 2 to 3 feet wide; CONDITIONS: prefers full sun with moist, well-drained soil; CARE: tolerates wet soil and part shade; PLANT PARTNERS: garden phlox, coneflowers, daisies; NOTES: plants will flop in too much shade and may grow aggressively in rich soil.

Shasta Daisy
(*Leucanthemum superbum*)

White-flowered daisies make a great addition to the evening garden. Their charming flowers top mounded plants that offer a nice contrast against vertical perennials like liatris and Culver's root. There are many cultivars available. Some, like 'Cream Puff' have yellow buds that open to creamy white flowers with a gold center. Snip off the spent flowers and you'll have a few months of continuous bloom. Because they can be short-lived perennials, I divide them about every three years.

COMMON NAMES: shasta daisy; **HARDINESS:** zones 5 to 9; **SIZE:** 14 to 20 inches tall and 24 to 28 inches wide; **CONDITIONS:** full sun; **CARE:** remove the spent flowers to encourage more blossoms; **PLANT PARTNERS:** vertical flowering perennials and annuals like liatris and salvia; **NOTES:** shasta daisies are not fussy about soil and they have low water needs.

Shasta daisies are all-time favorites for the white garden.

Calamint is one of the longest blooming perennials for the garden.

White Calamint
(*Calamintha nepeta* 'Montrose White')

Few perennials bloom for more than three or four weeks, but calamint blooms for a good three months or more—June through September—in our garden. It's a great perennial used in the front of a border and its delicate flowers attract hordes of pollinators. Because it is lightly scented, the deer that wander through our garden leave it alone. Ditto for bunnies.

COMMON NAMES: calamint; **HARDINESS:** zones 5 to 9 (in zones 7 through 9, plants may not perform well); **SIZE:** 1½ feet tall and wide; **CONDITIONS:** full sun and dry to medium-dry soils; **CARE:** cut back plants close to the ground after flowering to tidy the foliage and prevent self-sowing; **PLANT PARTNERS:** annuals, butterfly bush, coneflowers, roses; **NOTES:** foliage may decline in hot, humid weather.

Lamb's Ears (*Stachys byzantina*)

I love lamb's ears for their soft, velvety leaves that form a mat 6 to 9 inches off the ground. In the white garden, the silver leaves act as a foil for white-flowered plants. Well-drained soils are essential, otherwise plants may rot, especially if winter conditions are wet. There are cultivars, such as 'Helene Von Stein' and 'Big Ears' that have good summer foliage and rarely produce flowering stems. They also have leaves that are much larger than the straight species. Lamb's ears make a nice edging in front of a border or as a single specimen.

 COMMON NAMES: lamb's ears; **HARDINESS:** zones 4 to 8/9; **SIZE:** 1 to 1½ feet tall and wide; **CONDITIONS:** full sun and well-drained soil; **CARE:** plants may need dividing every 3 or so years; **PLANT PARTNERS:** calamint, coneflowers, roses, annuals; **NOTES:** if you use plants that produce flowers, clip the stems close to the ground to keep the foliage as the focal point.

Lamb's ear offers a silvery soft counterpoint to white flowers.

Silver Mound Artemisia (*Artemisia schmidtiana* 'Silver Mound')

This perennial is a showstopper with its silver, fine textured foliage. It's particularly stunning when planted in large drifts where it provides a wonderful contrast to plants with green foliage and white flowers. It's also great when used alone as an accent plant. It definitely prefers well-drained soil in full sun. It looks great with roses, lamb's ears, coneflowers, and other sun-loving perennials.

COMMON NAMES: silver mound artemisia, ghost plant; **HARDINESS:** zones 3 to 9; **SIZE:** 8 to 14 inches tall and wide; **CONDITIONS:** full sun and well-drained soil; **CARE:** can be sheared by half in summer if needed; **PLANT PARTNERS:** other drought-tolerant perennials and annuals; **NOTES:** allow soil to dry slightly before watering.

The glorious silver foliage is a nice contrast with large-leaved perennials.

Honorine Jobert Anemone
(*Anemone* x *hybrida* 'Honorine Jobert')

'Honorine Jobert' is an heirloom anemone cultivar discovered in France in 1858. It makes a great addition to the evening garden because it blooms from late summer into early fall when few perennials are blooming. Each flower is 2 to 3 inches wide, and they often bloom after the first fall frost. It can spread a bit, but it has not been aggressive or invasive in our garden because it's planted in a spot that has clay soil and has not been enriched with compost.

COMMON NAMES: Japanese anemone, windflower, thimble flower; **HARDINESS:** zones 4 to 8; **SIZE:** 3 to 4 feet tall and wide; can spread in ideal organic soils; **CONDITIONS:** full sun to part shade with evenly moist, rich soil; **CARE:** excess unwanted plants can be removed in spring; **PLANT PARTNERS:** white variegated hostas, joe pye weed, daisies, annuals; **NOTES:** provides nectar for late season pollinators.

This lovely late-flowering perennial extends the bloom season into fall.

The large, luminous blossoms of hardy hibiscus are like spotlights in the evening garden.

White Rose Mallow
(*Hibiscus* 'French Vanilla')

The cultivar 'French Vanilla' hails from a hardy North American plant. Like other perennial hibiscus, it boasts giant flowers. Although plants are slow to take off in spring, once they start flowering, they continue through autumn in our garden. They also attract bees and hummingbirds. Each flower lasts a day and makes a nice contrast against the dark foliage. There are many white-flowered cultivars available. The hardest part will be choosing one.

COMMON NAMES: rose mallow, hardy hibiscus; **HARDINESS:** zones 4 to 9; **SIZE:** 4 feet tall and wide; **CONDITIONS:** full sun and moist, well-drained soil; **CARE:** cut plants down in spring before new growth appears; **PLANT PARTNERS:** swamp milkweed, obedient plant, annuals; **NOTES:** remove spent flowers to keep plant looking neat.

Butterfly Bush (*Buddleia davidii*)

I've included butterfly bush in the perennials chapter, although it can also be considered a woody sub-shrub—one that dies back over winter, depending on the cold. Although *Buddleia* (aka *Buddleja*) can be invasive in some areas where it is quick to reseed, that has not been a problem in our Midwestern garden. *Buddleia* is one of the last plants blooming in September when we see monarch butterflies migrating and they flock to the blossoms for nectar. The flowers are very fragrant—like honey and vanilla. I cut the plants down in late winter to about 12 inches to produce strong growth. While most butterfly bushes are purple, violet, or pink, there are several white cultivars, like 'White Profusion', 'Dapper', and 'Pugster White'. Remove the spent flowers to encourage more blooms.

The butterfly bush, known for its long, spiked flowers, attracts a variety of pollinators and is especially favored by butterflies.

COMMON NAMES: butterfly bush; **HARDINESS:** zones 5 to 9; **SIZE:** from 2 to 7 feet tall and 2 to 6 feet wide; **CONDITIONS:** full sun and well-drained soil; does not tolerate cold, soggy soil; **CARE:** remove the seed heads to tidy up the plant; **PLANT PARTNERS:** coneflowers, liatris, annuals; **NOTES:** choose a site that is well-drained especially in winter so roots don't rot.

White-flowered coneflowers attract butterflies and other pollinators.

White Coneflower (*Echinacea purpurea* 'Alba')

Although our native coneflowers tend to be pink-purple (thus the species name '*purpurea*'), there are many cultivars in shades of yellow and orange and bicolored petals. But for the white garden, there's 'PowWow White', 'White Swan', 'Alba', and many other white-flowered cultivars. These handsome perennials have large, pure-white flowers with a prominent raised central cone. By August, I let the flowers develop seeds and leave the stems standing because they offer food for many birds, like goldfinches, over winter. When the snow sits on the dried dark cones, it's a lovely sight.

COMMON NAMES: white coneflower; **HARDINESS:** zones 3 to 8; **SIZE:** 18 to 24 inches tall and wide; **CONDITIONS:** full sun with moist, well-drained soil; **CARE:** in the summer, remove the spent flowers to encourage more blossoms; **PLANT PARTNERS:** liatris, daisies, salvia; **NOTES:** plants grown from the seeds may produce purple-pink flowers instead of white.

Bugbane (*Actaea simplex* 'Hillside Black Beauty')

For gardens in part to full shade, here is a plant that is not only easy to grow, but is a stunner when it sends up tall fluffy spires of fragrant white flowers in September and October. The architectural height is a good contrast for low, mounding plants like hostas, hellebores and epimedium. The cultivar 'Hillside Black Beauty' offers coppery-purple foliage, a nice contrast to the flowers.

COMMON NAMES: bugbane, cohosh; **HARDINESS:** zones 4 to 8; **SIZE:** 4 to 6 feet tall and 3 to 4 feet wide; foliage forms a clump 2½ feet tall; **CONDITIONS:** part to full shade, moist organic soil; **CARE:** site in location out of strong wind; **PLANT PARTNERS:** other shade-loving perennials and native wildflowers; **NOTES:** in substantial shade, flowering stems may bend toward light.

Tall spires of creamy white fragrant flowers appear in autumn.

Goat's beard offers fine-textured foliage and early summer blossoms.

Goat's Beard (*Aruncus dioicus*)

This Midwestern native perennial thrives in moist woodlands. It forms a tall clump of dark green foliage with astilbe-like flowers that rise above the leaves to create a bold effect. There are several cultivars including the dwarf goat's beard *A. aethusifolius* 'Misty Lace', which grows 1½ to 2 feet tall and wide, making it a good choice for the front of a border.

COMMON NAMES: goat's beard; **HARDINESS:** zones 4 to 8; **SIZE:** 1½ to 4 feet tall and wide depending on the cultivar; **CONDITIONS:** full sun to part shade; prefers moist soils; foliage can decline in dry soil; **CARE:** remove the faded blooms to improve the plant's appearance; **PLANT PARTNERS:** rose mallow, bugbane; **NOTES:** if you like the look of the dried flowers, there's no need to remove them.

Bridal Veil Astilbe
(*Astilbe* x *arendsii* 'Bridal Veil')

There are many types of astilbes in all sorts of colors and heights, but the cultivars with white-flowered feathery plumes brighten the evening garden. Although they grow best in part shade, you can grow astilbe in full sun in the morning, providing there is afternoon shade. Use them in drifts or as a specimen plant. Before planting, I add compost to enrich the soil and I always keep them watered, especially during periods of drought.

> **COMMON NAMES:** astilbe, false spirea; **HARDINESS:** zones 4 to 8; **SIZE:** depending on the cultivar, anywhere from 10 inches to 4 feet tall and 1 to 4 feet wide; **CONDITIONS:** part shade with rich moist soil; **CARE:** water during dry periods; **PLANT PARTNERS:** other shade- and moisture-loving perennials; **NOTES:** can be divided every 3 to 5 years.

Astilbe's fernlike leaves and plumes of flowers offer a counterpoint to bold-leaved perennials.

White gardens in shade benefit from the silver-white leaves of Japanese painted ferns.

Japanese Painted Fern
(*Athyrium niponicum*)

Japanese painted ferns, with their dramatic foliage, stand out in the shade garden. Slow spreading, these ferns can have silver and burgundy tones and wonderful textures. The cultivar 'Pictum' has luminous silver-green fronds with a dark central rib. They are slow-growing and clump-forming and work well with spring-blooming flowers like white daffodils and native wildflowers. Pair them with plants that have bold-textured leaves like coral bells and hostas.

> **COMMON NAMES:** Japanese painted fern, ghost fern; **HARDINESS:** zones 5 to 8; **SIZE:** 18 to 24 inches tall and wide (the cultivar 'Godzilla' can be 3 feet tall); **CONDITIONS:** part to full shade with moist organic soil; **CARE:** remove the dried stems in late winter before new growth resumes; **PLANT PARTNERS:** other shade- and moisture-loving perennials (coral bells, lungwort, hosta); **NOTES:** easy care, but prefers moderate, consistent moisture.

Hosta (*Hosta*)

Hostas are shade-loving perennials known for their lush foliage, which comes in various colors and patterns, and their ability to thrive in low-light conditions.

In many regions, hostas are the cornerstone of the shade garden. Some, like August lily (*H. plantaginea*), have very fragrant white flowers over bright green quilted leaves. Its trumpet-shaped white flowers rise up on 30-inch-tall scapes. Look for plants that have white or creamy yellow and blue-green foliage. The variegation helps light up the white garden in shade.

COMMON NAMES: hosta, plantain lily; **HARDINESS:** zones 3 to 9; **SIZE:** depending on the cultivar anywhere from 6 to 60 inches tall and 12 to 72 inches wide; **CONDITIONS:** part to full shade; moist, well-drained fertile soil; **CARE:** divide plants (if needed) in spring when new growth is about 6 inches tall; **PLANT PARTNERS:** coral bells, Japanese painted ferns, Japanese forest grass (*Hakonechloa*), bugbane; **NOTES:** hostas look great with fine-textured perennials like ferns.

Perennial Forget-Me-Not (*Brunnera macrophylla*)

When it comes to shade, there's more to color than flowers. *Brunnera*, the perennial forget-me-not, has cultivars with wonderful, variegated silver and gray-green heart-shaped foliage. Some cultivars have bright streaks and patches in the leaves. This is a perennial that looks good against the wide leaves of hostas as well as fine-textured ferns. Too much sun or not enough water can lead to browning on leaf tips. Tiny sprays of pale blue flowers appear in spring. Look for 'Jack Frost', 'Dawson's White', 'Hadspen Cream', 'Alexander's Great', 'Sea Heart', and 'Silver Heart'.

COMMON NAMES: Siberian bugloss, perennial forget-me-not; **HARDINESS:** zones 3 to 7; **SIZE:** 1 to 2 feet tall and 2 to 3 feet wide; **CONDITIONS:** part shade; **CARE:** give them a shady site with moist (not soggy) soil; remove spent flowers; **PLANT PARTNERS:** hostas, ferns, astilbe, dwarf goat's beard; **NOTES:** plants prefer cool summers; will not perform well in hot, humid conditions (zones 8-9).

The wonderfully variegated leaves of *Brunnera* cultivars add interest to the white shade garden.

Tall garden phlox is a long-time favorite in cottage gardens.

Garden Phlox (*Phlox paniculata* 'David')

Unlike ground-hugging, creeping phlox, tall garden phlox produces large clusters of flowers. There are several white-flowered cultivars and some that are white with a pink center. The cultivar 'David' offers enormous heads of fragrant white flowers, but even more important, it is very resistant to powdery mildew, which often plagues other garden phlox. Look for other cultivars including 'Backlight', 'Jade', and 'Flame White'.

COMMON NAMES: garden phlox; **HARDINESS:** zones 4 to 8; **SIZE:** 18 to 24 inches tall and wide; **CONDITIONS:** prefers full sun; will tolerate some afternoon shade; **CARE:** remove spent flowers to prevent self-sowing; **PLANT PARTNERS:** liatris, coneflower, culver's root; **NOTES:** attracts butterflies and other pollinators.

Culver's root (*Veronicastrum virginicum*)

I love this native perennial for the candelabra-like flowers that float above the leaves. Although it prefers wet soils, I've grown Culver's root in good garden soil with average moisture. In warm, Southern states, it benefits from afternoon shade, but in Northern climates, it thrives in full sun. Too much shade and the plant tends to flop. It's another perennial that offers a strong vertical accent and contrast against daisy-type blossoms.

COMMON NAMES: culver's root, bowman's root; **HARDINESS:** zones 3 to 8; **SIZE:** 3 to 5 feet tall (or more) and 2 to 4 feet wide; **CONDITIONS:** full sun and moist soil; tolerates wet soil; **CARE:** remove the spent blossoms to extend flowering period; **PLANT PARTNERS:** coneflowers, daisies, phlox; **NOTES:** a low maintenance, native perennial that attracts pollinators.

Culver's root is native to Northeastern North America.

Chapter 8

Shrubs and Roses

Shrubs are the backbone of the garden. They can provide structure, flowers, and multi-season interest. They are useful when a less-than-desirable view (the neighbor's garbage cans, for example) needs screening. When annuals, perennials, and vines are finished blooming, deciduous shrubs (those that lose their leaves in fall) provide winter interest with their twiggy stems and different shapes. I've included roses in this chapter because many of the newer shrub-type varieties are disease-resistant and repeat bloomers.

Shrubs, sometimes called bushes, are small- to medium-size woody plants with multiple stems that tend to be under 15 feet tall. Some shrubs, like panicle hydrangeas, are trained to grow into a single stem, called a standard. Sub-shrubs are low-growing shrubs or woody perennials, like lavender, butterfly bush, hardy hibiscus, and Russian sage, usually under 1½ feet tall and not more than 3 feet tall when mature. Sub-shrubs often die back to the ground in colder climates in fall and resume growth in spring.

Whatever shrubs you choose for your white garden, consider how much space you have. You want a plant to fit the allotted space without constant pruning to keep it in bounds. This will save you a lot of time and aggravation in the future. When choosing shrubs, I look at how many seasons of interest the plant offers. When does it bloom? Are the flowers fragrant? Is it susceptible to a host of insects or diseases? Will it need frequent pruning to look good? How much sun or shade will it need to thrive? The answers will prevent you from planting a less-than-desirable shrub or having to replace one down the road.

Shrubs are an essential part of the white garden.

Rose of Sharon (*Hibiscus syriacus*) blooms for several weeks.

Shrubs can be upright, mounded, arching, and vase-shaped.

Because they produce several stems, shrubs sometimes require pruning to look their best. Some overgrown shrubs respond to rejuvenation pruning—removing the oldest, thickest stems as close to the ground as possible. This stimulates new shoots to emerge just below the pruning cut. If you simply trim the shrub into a ball, you won't enjoy its natural shape, and this may produce tall, "leggy" plants. Shrubs that respond to rejuvenation pruning include lilac, spirea, weigela, flowering quince, deutzia, mock orange, forsythia, red-stemmed dogwood, and butterfly bush. I cut down our butterfly bushes in early spring to about 12 inches above ground before the leaves emerge. This produces a plant with many sturdy stems and plenty of flowers because the blooms develop on new wood.

Overgrown shrubs can also be pruned gradually over a three-year period, a process called renewal pruning. One-third of the old stems are removed each year, so that by year three, the plant will have produced all new growth. This allows more light and air into the shrub's center and encourages new growth at the base. The result is better flowering, a better shape, and a more manageable size. Shrubs that respond well to renewal pruning include flowering almond, chokeberry (*Aronia*), potentilla, cotoneaster, deutzia, gray dogwood, red-stemmed dogwoods, lilac, forsythia, flowering quince, rhododendrons and azaleas, spirea, weigela, witch hazel and viburnum.

If you must prune a shrub, think about when it blooms. Spring-flowering shrubs are best pruned right after they have finished flowering. Summer-flowering shrubs are pruned before spring growth begins. Panicle hydrangeas are an example of a summer-flowering shrub. The flowers develop on stems that grow during the spring and summer.

The following are some of the shrubs that I've grown or have admired in other gardens.

Pink buds open to fragrant, creamy white flowers.

Fragrant Viburnums (*Viburnum spp.*)

There are native and non-native *Viburnums*, and I grow both. But it's the fragrant Koreanspice (*V. carlesii*) and Judd (*V.* x *juddii*) that I adore for their spring fragrance and delightful fall colors. Along one side border, I grow a large Koreanspice that starts blooming in May, its almond-vanilla fragrance filling the air on a warm day. It blooms about the same time as our white-flowered fringe tree (*Chionanthus virginicus*) and star magnolia, all underplanted with white daffodils. The Judd viburnum grows in the same border and starts with pink buds that open to snowball clusters of fragrant white blooms in the spring. But it's the fall color—reds and purples—that make this shrub a multi-season delight. Another favorite is Spice Girl® with its large flower clusters and a spicy-sweet scent in mid-spring. It reaches 6 to 7 feet tall and wide.

Place fragrant *Viburnums* where you can enjoy their scent in late spring and early summer.

COMMON NAMES: Koreanspice viburnum, Korean viburnum, Judd viburnum; **HARDINESS:** zones 4 to 8 depending on species or cultivar; **SIZE:** 4 to 8 feet depending on the cultivar; **CONDITIONS:** moist well-drained soils in full to part sun; **CARE:** relatively trouble free, although leaf spots and borers are possible problems; **PLANT PARTNERS:** other flowering shrubs and small ornamental trees; **NOTES:** use as a specimen plant, in a border, on a foundation, or in a mass planting.

Chokeberry (*Aronia spp.*)

Red and black chokeberries are native to North America. They can reach 4 to 8 feet in height, but there are cultivars that are much more compact, such as Low Scape Mound®, a black chokeberry that reaches 1 to 2 feet tall and 1½ to 2 feet wide. The cultivar 'Morton' (Iroquois Beauty™) is also compact at 2 to 3 feet tall. These multi-stemmed shrubs can form large, dense colonies over time.

Black chokeberry (*A. melanocarpa*) produces clusters of small, white flowers in mid-spring. They are followed by small, dark purple to black fruit in late summer and autumn. Red chokeberry (*A. arbutifolia*) is a tall, multi-stemmed shrub with abundant white flowers, red glossy berries, and outstanding red fall color. Both are tough, dependable plants with three-season interest, and are useful for shady, wet sites, but they tolerate dry soils, too. They work well in either a formal white garden or a naturalized landscape. The red chokeberry cultivar, 'Brilliantissima', flowers abundantly with large fruits and brilliant red autumn color on plants that are 6 to 10 feet tall and 3 to 5 feet wide.

Native chokeberries offer fragrance and multi-season interest.

COMMON NAMES: black chokeberry, red chokeberry; **HARDINESS:** zones 4 to 9; **SIZE:** depending on cultivar, plants can be 1 to 10 feet tall and 2 to 5 feet wide; **CONDITIONS:** Full sun to part shade. Tolerates both wet and dry sites; prefers acidic soil; **CARE:** Blooms on old wood. Lightly shape plants as needed in late winter or after flowering; **PLANT PARTNERS:** use in a hedge, a foundation planting or with other native plants; **NOTES:** Multi-stemmed with suckers; stems are upright, and the shrub tends to form broad thickets. If needed, remove suckers (rooting branches) to prevent spreading.

Low Scape Mound® black chokeberry works well in small spaces.

Many panicle hydrangea flowers turn pale to deep pink in late summer.

Panicle Hydrangea (*Hydrangea paniculata*)

If there was a beauty contest for flowering shrubs, surely the panicle hydrangea would come in first place. In recent years, a bevy of new hydrangeas have appeared in garden centers and catalogs. Breeders have been busy introducing cultivars of the panicle hydrangeas (*H. paniculata*) in a variety of sizes with upright cone-shaped flowers, like those of 'Vanilla Strawberry' and 'Quick Fire' that turn from creamy white to blushing pink in late summer. They make a stunning addition to a white garden, in a foundation planting, a hedge, as a specimen in very large containers, or in a mixed border of shrubs and perennials.

Giant pale panicle hydrangea blossoms are like beacons in the evening garden.

COMMON NAMES: panicle hydrangea; **HARDINESS:** zones 3 to 8; **SIZE:** 3 feet tall and wide for dwarf cultivars like 'Bobo' and as much as 15 feet tall and 12 feet wide for others; **CONDITIONS:** full to part sun in rich, moist, well-drained soil; **CARE:** leave the spent flowers for winter interest but remove them before spring growth begins; **PLANT PARTNERS:** variegated sedum, white coneflowers, ornamental grasses; **NOTES:** adaptable to many soils, moderate moisture required.

'Annabelle' is a selection of the native smooth hydrangea found growing in Anna, Illinois.

Smooth Hydrangea
(*Hydrangea arborescens*)

Annabelle Hydrangea (*Hydrangea arborescens* 'Annabelle') is a long-time favorite in our garden. Its large, creamy flowers light up the beds on both sides of our driveway. The flowers are anywhere from 6 to 12 inches wide, about the size of a softball. The hydrangea was first discovered in Anna, Illinois, more than a century ago. In its native habitat, the straight species features small, flat flowers. In the garden, smooth hydrangeas spread slowly, sending up new stems each spring until they make a rather enormous clump. The stems can be cut down to 6 or 8 inches in late winter because the flowers bloom on the current year's growth. It's a whopper of a plant, and a newer cultivar, Incrediball®, has even larger flowers with strong, sturdy stems. Flowering begins in mid-summer produces enormous "summer snowballs."

COMMON NAMES: smooth hydrangea; **HARDINESS:** zones 3 to 8; **SIZE:** 4 to 5 feet tall and wide; spread slowly by suckering; **CONDITIONS:** moist but not soggy soil; shade to part sun; **CARE:** cut flowering stems close to the ground in late winter or early spring; **PLANT PARTNERS:** white coneflowers, liatris, other white-flowering perennials; **NOTES:** plants may wilt on hot, dry days but recover in the evening.

'Incrediball' is a cultivar with enormous flowers on sturdy stems.

Tree Peony (*Paeonia suffruticosa*)

One of my favorite shrubs is the tree peony with its large, crepe-paper blossoms. Unlike older, herbaceous peonies that die down to the ground each fall, tree peonies have woody stems and rarely need pruning. The flower buds develop on the previous year's stems so if you prune in spring, you will lose blossoms. They grow in part shade in our woodland garden and on the east side of our house where they get morning sun and afternoon shade. When grown in full sun, the blossoms will not last as long especially if the spring weather is warm or hot.

COMMON NAMES: tree peony; **HARDINESS:** zones 4 to 9; **SIZE:** 2 to 5 feet tall and wide; **CONDITIONS:** part sun (morning sun preferable); sandy loam; tree peonies cannot tolerate wet feet; **CARE:** many tree peonies have grafted roots that should be buried below the soil surface when planting; **PLANT PARTNERS:** spring-blooming bulbs, roses, azaleas, hydrangeas; **NOTES:** choose a spot away from the roots of large trees or shrubs.

The tree peony's flowers attract many pollinators in spring.

Variegated Red-Twig Dogwood (*Cornus alba* 'Elegantissima')

One way to light up a shade garden without using white flowers is with variegated foliage like that of 'Elegantissima' and 'Ivory Halo' shrubby dogwood. Although some gardeners say the variegation is more pronounced in full sun, the leaves are nicely white and green in dappled shade. The green and white leaves, white flowers, attractive berries, good fall color and red stems make it a multi-season performer. I cut back thick, older stems to within two or three buds (side shoots) at the base in early spring. This allows the younger red stems to shine through in winter.

COMMON NAMES: red-twig dogwood, variegated dogwood; **HARDINESS:** zones 2 to 8; **SIZE:** 6 to 10 feet tall and wide; **CONDITIONS:** full sun to part shade; moist soil; **CARE:** water during periods of drought; **PLANT PARTNERS:** moisture-loving perennials and shrubs; **NOTES:** the flowers are faintly fragrant.

Variegated red-twig dogwood offers attractive foliage in the white garden.

New disease-resistant shrub roses offer repeat blooms throughout the growing season.

Roses (*Rosa spp.*)

What's not to like about roses? Well, the older hybrid tea roses were a lot of work—spraying to keep insects and fungal diseases from disfiguring the leaves and buds. Most gardeners didn't enjoy that type of maintenance. However, there are many new cultivars that have been bred for disease-resistance and repeat bloom. Shrub roses like 'White Simplicity', 'Snowcone', and 'Pure Perfume' offer dark green glossy foliage and lightly sweet flowers. 'Wedding Dress' is a ground cover rose that reaches 2 feet tall and 3 feet wide, and as the name suggests, it is covered with 2-inch-wide, pure white flowers that have a spicy fragrance.

Shrub roses can be used in drifts or as a specimen plant.

COMMON NAMES: shrub rose, ground cover rose; **HARDINESS:** zones 5 to 9; **SIZE:** 2 to 5 feet tall and wide depending on the cultivar; **CONDITIONS:** full sun, moist, well-drained soil; **CARE:** provide a granular fertilizer around the base of the plant in spring; **PLANT PARTNERS:** liatris, coneflowers, daisies, culver's root; **NOTES:** remove dead/dried stems in late winter.

Ground cover roses are low-growing plants that can be used at the front of a white border.

Slender Deutzia (*Deutzia gracilis*)

Deutzia is a wonderful small shrub with pretty, double white flowers in late spring. The slender, arching stems produce fragrant, bell-shaped flowers. Stems occasionally die back and can be removed in winter or early spring. Plants tend to be deer-resistant and tolerant of clay soils. This delightful shrub can be used as an informal hedge or mixed in a white-garden border or foundation planting.

COMMON NAMES: slender deutzia; **HARDINESS:** zones 5 to 8; **SIZE:** 2 to 5 feet tall and wide; **CONDITIONS:** full sun; afternoon shade in warm regions; moist humus-rich soil; **CARE:** flower buds develop on the previous year's growth so prune immediately after flowering, if needed; **PLANT PARTNERS:** shasta daisies, siberian iris, roses; **NOTES:** Chardonnay Pearls® 'Duncan' slender deutzia offers lemon-lime foliage.

Slender deutzia produces a profusion of bell-shaped flowers in spring.

Snowmound spirea offers a fountain of flowers.

Spirea (*Spiraea nipponica*)

Spirea shrubs, especially the old-fashioned bridal-wreath spirea, were a favorite of the Victorians. Homeowners used the large arching shrubs to cover tall foundations with their sprays of white flowers and delicate leaves. 'Snowmound' spirea (*Spiraea nipponica* 'Snowmound') is an easy to grow shrub with graceful, spreading branches, dark green leaves, and abundant clusters of white flowers that provide a spectacular show in spring. 'Snowmound' is smaller than the straight species and typically grows 3 to 4 feet tall and wide.

COMMON NAMES: 'Snowmound' spirea, bridal-wreath spirea; **HARDINESS:** zones 4 to 8; **SIZE:** 3 to 5 feet tall and wide or more depending on the cultivar; **CONDITIONS:** full to part sun; appreciates light afternoon shade in hot summer climates; **CARE:** a light shearing will remove faded flowers; **PLANT PARTNERS:** viburnum, roses; **NOTES:** flowers on new wood so pruning can be done in late winter if needed.

Lilac (*Syringa vulgaris*)

Lilacs have long been admired for their intense fragrance in late spring. Although there are many pink, magenta, light blue, and violet lilac flowers, white-flowered cultivars can add fragrance to your white garden bed or border. Older varieties of common lilac (*Syringa vulgaris*) are susceptible to mildew on the foliage and they tend to be very large shrubs. Breeders have created new cultivars that are compact and suitable in a border or as a hedge. 'New Age' lilac is 4 to 6 feet tall and wide, mildew-resistant and has a lovely fragrance. 'Angel White' offers large clusters of fragrant, pure-white flowers produced without winter chilling, which is usually needed for most common lilacs. It will perform better in regions with warmer winters.

COMMON NAMES: lilac; **HARDINESS:** zones 3 to 7; **SIZE:** common lilacs may be 8 to 12 feet tall and wide; there are several compact cultivars suitable for small gardens; **CONDITIONS:** full sun but will tolerate some light shade; **CARE:** water when the top 2 inches of soil feels dry; **PLANT PARTNERS:** peonies, ornamental grasses, viburnum; **NOTES:** cut spent flowers when the petals fade.

The fragrance and flowers of white lilacs fill the garden in May.

New, bright leaves on 'Hakuro Nishiki' willow provide a wonderful contrast in the white garden.

Hakuro Nishiki Variegated Willow (*Salix integra* 'Hakuro Nishiki')

This shrubby willow is grown for its foliage rather than the flowers. I've grown Nishiki willow in both full sun and part shade and love it in spring when it becomes a fountain of light-colored foliage. The new leaves are a combination of blue-green, white and pink on slender, arching red branches. Once summer is in full swing, the foliage turns more green. This willow is occasionally grown with one trunk, as a standard. I renewal prune our shrubs in late winter or early spring to encourage vigorous growth and to control plant size. A mature plant can take up a lot of room! If you prefer a large shrub, then no pruning is needed.

COMMON NAMES: Nishiki willow, Japanese dappled willow; **HARDINESS:** zones 4 to 9; **SIZE:** 5 to 7 feet tall and wide; **CONDITIONS:** full sun to part shade and moist, fertile soil; **CARE:** thrives in consistently moist soils; **PLANT PARTNERS:** hostas, carex; **NOTES:** can be used at the edge of a pond or stream or in a shrub border.

Chapter 9
Annual and Perennial Vines: Upward and Onward

Vertical elements like arbors, trellises, and obelisks are very useful in narrow planting beds where it's difficult to get height and coverage with shrubs or other plants. That's where flowering vines come in handy.

Annual vines like moonflower and hyacinth bean are useful if you're trying to quickly cover a structure or a fence. You can collect the dried seeds and sow them the next year and send the rest of the dried vines to the compost pile. Because they are annuals, they flower, set seed, and die at the end of the growing season, which allows you to grow something else in their place the following year, if desired. Perennial vines like climbing hydrangea and clematis grow larger each year. Grow an annual and perennial vine together and they will twine gracefully skyward, providing flowers and interest in the white garden throughout the growing season.

A trellis placed against a wall or fence takes up little space. In some urban settings or on small lots, a planting bed may be shallow—only two feet wide or so. This is where a vine-covered trellis becomes invaluable. It can create a focal point and it gives you more space in which to garden.

You can find trellises at garden centers, big box stores, and online. If you have something special or unique in mind, talk with a landscaper or carpenter. Look for products made with long-lasting materials, such as rot-resistant cedar or fir, heavy-duty resin, or powder-coated metal. For screening purposes, a trellis panel may feature horizontal and vertical or diamond-shaped cross bars placed close to one another to screen a view. Others may have more open cross bars allowing the vines to scramble through and up both sides. Vines can also cover chain link and cast-iron fences or poles.

Vines add height, especially in tight spaces.

An arbor is a perfect support for flowering vines.

Some vines, like ivy, have roots that attach to a wall.

Vines grow by twining—wrapping their stems around a vertical object, by tendrils (modified stems or leaves), or by clinging rootlets along the stem that attach themselves to the support. Some, like those of climbing hydrangea, have adhesive discs, called holdfasts, on the roots that stick to the support. Avoid damage to buildings by keeping rootlet-type vines away from brick and mortar or wood structures. If you plan on attaching a trellis to a wall, it should be easy to remove if you need to make repairs.

Twining vines usually need some encouragement to wrap around their support. When growing vines on a lamp post, for example, you may need to place netting, string, or wire from the top to the bottom to give tendrils and stems something to wrap around.

Obelisks and tuteurs are handy for growing smaller vines like cypress vine and black-eyed Susan vine. The typical shape is a four-sided, tall and rounded upright form. Tuteurs tend to be three-sided like a pyramid, wider at the base than at the top.

When choosing a trellis or arbor, take a cue from your home's architecture. Look at the windows for design clues. You may want the trellis style to match mullions in the windowpanes or have a curve if the window frames are arched. Or, if you live in a mid-century modern ranch, you may want a more contemporary metal, rust-resistant structure. Vines can scramble up a deck railing or you can use them in a large pot with an obelisk for support. A pergola (an extended arbor) over a patio or in a side yard is another elegant structure on which to grow vines. Bamboo poles are another way to support annual vines. Place poles about 6 to 8 inches into the ground and secure them at the top with twine.

Tendrils need a support on which to twine.

Annual vines scramble up this bamboo structure.

Vines can be used on just about any support.

Moonflower Vine (*Ipomoea alba*)

One of the most fascinating vines is the moonflower, which quickly unfurls at dusk to attract evening pollinators. The trumpet-shaped flowers are 3 to 6 inches across and have a jasmine scent. Plant them near a patio, deck, or walkway where they can be enjoyed on a summer evening. Each flower stays open until early morning. If you live in a colder climate, sow seeds in spring outdoors after the last frost date for your area. Seedlings emerge in 7 to 14 days and the plant blooms in late summer to fall. For earlier bloom, sow seeds indoors 2 to 4 weeks before the last spring frost in your region. To aid germination, soak the seeds in water for five or six hours. Vines really get going in hot weather and can grow anywhere from 6 to 20 feet—big, bold, and magical!

Spectacular fragrant blossoms twirl open at dusk.

COMMON NAMES: moonflower, moonvine, night-blooming morning glory; **HARDINESS:** annual (sensitive to cold and frost); **SIZE:** 8 to 20 feet; climbs by twining; **CONDITIONS:** full sun, average moisture; **CARE:** over-fertilizing will produce more foliage at the expense of flowers; **PLANT PARTNERS:** morning glories, cypress vine, painted lady runner beans; **NOTES:** collect the dried seeds in fall for future planting and store in a frost-free spot.

White hyacinth bean grows quickly in warm weather.

White Hyacinth Bean (*Dolichos lablab* 'Alba' or 'Silver Moon')

This lovely heirloom was introduced from Japan in the 1860s. An annual vine, it produces heart-shaped leaves and prolific, pea-like flowers. It's a workhorse in the evening garden, but the blooms remain open day and night. Each wand of slightly fragrant flowers lasts several days. A fast-growing climber, white hyacinth bean quickly reaches 15 feet or more in a single season. The cultivar 'Silver Moon' can reach 20 feet by summer's end. Warm weather and a sunny location encourage an ongoing crop of flowers and seed pods. This cottage garden charmer is great for covering walls, trellises, arbors, fences, or porch railings.

COMMON NAMES: hyacinth bean, lablab bean; **HARDINESS:** annual; **SIZE:** 6 to 20 feet; climbs by twining; **CONDITIONS:** full sun and rich, moist, well-drained soil; **CARE:** amend the soil with organic matter before sowing seeds; **PLANT PARTNERS:** corkscrew vine, morning glories, purple hyacinth bean; **NOTES:** a vigorous twiner, white hyacinth bean needs a sturdy support.

White-flowered cypress vine offers many tiny, delicate flowers.

Cypress Vine
(*Ipomoea quamoclit* 'White')

This carefree vine produces fernlike foliage and masses of five-pointed small white flowers. Like its red- and pink-flowered cypress vine counterparts, this one also attracts hummingbirds. Grow it on a fence, a trellis or obelisk where it will quickly create a lacy blanket of foliage. The delicate leaves may curl on bright sunny days. Once it starts blooming, it continues producing flowers until fall frost in colder areas.

COMMON NAMES: white cypress vine; **HARDINESS:** zones 8 to 10; **SIZE:** 6 to 10 feet; **CONDITIONS:** full sun and good drainage; **CARE:** low maintenance, minimal care; **PLANT PARTNERS:** best grown alone so you can enjoy the foliage and flowers; **NOTES:** soaking seeds 12 to 24 hours aids in germination.

The intricacy of white-cypress vine adds visual interest to any garden.

Baby Boo Pumpkin

This sweet little vine produces 3-inch-wide white pumpkins on well-behaved plants and is easy to train on a trellis, tuteur, or obelisk. Vines grow about 4 to 5 feet and produce up to 10 pumpkins per plant. The white fruits extend the season of interest in your white garden. Sow seeds when the soil is warm—at least 60° F. Fruits take about 95 days from the time the seeds germinate to harvest.

> **COMMON NAMES:** miniature pumpkin, Mini White Pumpkin, Baby Boo; **HARDINESS:** annual; **SIZE:** 4 to 5 feet tall; climbs by twining; **CONDITIONS:** full sun, well-drained soil; **CARE:** provide supplemental water during dry weather to keep the vines healthy. Deep soakings are better than a light frequent watering; **PLANT PARTNERS:** other miniature gourds or pumpkins; **NOTES:** watch for squash bugs.

These miniature white pumpkins add a lovely touch to the white garden.

Climbing hydrangea offers fragrant lacy flowers and winter interest.

Climbing Hydrangea (*Hydrangea anomala* ssp. *petiolaris*)

This handsome, long-lived woody vine clings and climbs by means of tiny rootlets that attach to a wall, trellis, or other support. In midsummer, it is covered with lacy clusters of lightly fragrant, tiny white flowers, 6 to 10 inches wide, that contrast with the glossy green leaves. The horizontal branching pattern offers a sculptural effect against a wall, and the cinnamon-brown bark on older stems peels to create an interesting texture that is attractive in winter. Over the course of years, it may reach 30 feet or more. This vine uses root-like "holdfasts" that will grasp wood, brick, and mortar, so keep that in mind when placing plants on walls that may need painting or mortar repair in the future.

> **COMMON NAMES:** climbing hydrangea; **HARDINESS:** zones 5 to 9; **SIZE:** very slow to get growing the first five years; mature plants reach 30-plus feet; **CONDITIONS:** tolerates a range of light from full sun to full shade; moist, well-drained soil; **CARE:** add a layer of compost around the base of the plant each year; **PLANT PARTNERS:** best grown alone; **NOTES:** prune only as needed to control size and direction.

Twining snapdragon has been popular for more than a century.

Twining Snapdragon
(*Asarina scandens*)

This delicate vine was a favorite of Victorian-era gardeners. One of the best long-blooming annual vines, twining snapdragon blooms summer to fall with a profusion of sweet little trumpets that attract pollinators and hummingbirds. Use it alone on a trellis or in a container with an obelisk, or in window boxes on a deck railing where the vines will cascade down. Climbs by twining and wrapping leaf stalks around an object. Native to Mexico and southwestern United States.

COMMON NAMES: twining snapdragon, climbing snapdragon; **HARDINESS:** zones 8 to 10; **SIZE:** 6 to 8 feet; **CONDITIONS:** full sun to part shade; **CARE:** use a water-soluble fertilizer to promote flowering; **PLANT PARTNERS:** does well on its own; **NOTES:** can be grown in a large container with an obelisk or trellis.

Black-eyed Susan Vine
(*Thunbergia alata* 'Alba')

Native to tropical Africa, this annual vine can be used in window boxes and hanging baskets where its stems and flowers trail down. It is very easy to grow from seeds that can be started indoors in spring or outdoors after the last frost date for your area (if applicable). Its common name, "clock vine," refers to the way it twines its stems to the right. The cultivars 'Alba' and 'Bakeri' sport white flowers. This fast-growing vine does particularly well in hot, steamy weather.

COMMON NAMES: black-eyed Susan vine, clock vine; **HARDINESS:** zones 8 to 10 (tender perennial); **SIZE:** 5 to 8 feet; **CONDITIONS:** full sun to part shade with moderate moisture; **CARE:** seedlings resent root disturbance. If starting plants indoors, use peat pots that can go directly into the ground after spring frosts; **PLANT PARTNERS:** use them to trail from baskets or climb on a trellis; **NOTES:** Tolerates humidity and heat. Plants are sensitive to light frosts.

Dainty white flowers dot *Thunbergia alata* 'Alba'.

Clematis (*Clematis*)

The Queen of Vines lives up to its name.

It's no wonder that clematis is often called the queen of flowering vines. The flowers can be as large as 6 inches across. Most clematis are unsurpassed in their long bloom period. There are many large-flowered white cultivars like 'Candida', 'Henryi', 'Aagasumi', 'Jackmannii Alba', 'Miss Bateman', 'Blue Moon', 'Mrs. George Jackman', and 'Duchess of Edinburgh' to the small, delicate and fragrant blossoms on sweet autumn clematis (*C. Terniflora*).

Growing clematis can be a bit confusing because different types are pruned at different times of the year. There are three groups of clematis when it comes to pruning. Small-flowered, spring-blooming varieties such as *Clematis montana*, *C. macropetala*, and *C. alpina* belong to **Group 1**. Those in this group only need pruning when they outgrow their space. In that case, just cut out sufficient branches to clean up the plant.

Clematis in **Group 2** bloom in early or midsummer and typically have large flowers. Examples include 'Duchess of Edinburgh' and 'Beautiful Bride'. These need a bit more care and attention to get the most out of the flowers. Without pruning, they become leggy, and all the flowers will appear at the very top of the stems and not along the middle or bottom. Pruning should reduce the number of shoots but leave much of the older wood. This can be done right after the plant has finished flowering or in late winter before new growth begins.

There are numerous white-flowered clematis with tiny to large blossoms.

Clematis cultivars in **Group 3** include 'Summer Snow,' 'Sweet Sensation', and sweet autumn clematis, among others. The flowers appear on the current year's growth so all the vines can be cut back in midwinter to the first pair of healthy buds (side shoots) just above the ground.

Clematis vines prefer rich, organic soil with their roots shaded to keep them cool and the foliage and flowers getting the sun. Adding mulch or planting perennials near the base of the vine can help shade the roots. Besides growing these perennial vines on an arbor or trellis, they can be left on the ground to scramble over retaining walls or boulders.

COMMON NAMES: virgin's bower, old man's beard, traveler's joy; **HARDINESS:** zones 4 to 9 depending on species; **SIZE:** 6 to 12 feet or more depending on cultivar; **CONDITIONS:** Full to part sun in moist, well-drained soil. The vines like sunlight but the roots prefer to be cool. Achieve this by shading the base with other plants or adding a layer of mulch or pebbles at the base; **CARE:** Clematis are heavy feeders. Mulch with compost in the spring; **PLANT PARTNERS:** roses, lavender, catmint, phlox, dianthus; **NOTES:** add organic material (compost) and amend the soil before planting.

Sweet autumn clematis has a gorgeous, sweet fragrance.

Golden Hops Vine
(*Humulus lupulus* 'Aurea')

This vine is unique because of its bright chartreuse foliage and climbing over an arbor it reflects light at dusk. It's valuable for its quick foliage effect in spring and early summer and is particularly striking against a dark green or purple background. I grow it on a purple metal arbor where its tiny "hops" dangle overhead. Hops grow in sun or shade, but the foliage will be more vivid when grown in full sun.

COMMON NAMES: golden hop vine, hops vine; HARDINESS: zones 3 to 8; SIZE: 10 to 18 feet during the season; climbs by twining; CONDITIONS: full sun to light shade; foliage is more striking in full sun; needs good drainage; CARE: remove old stems before the new growth starts in spring; PLANT PARTNERS: clematis, moonflower.

The chartreuse leaves add interest to the white garden.

Delicate fragrant flowers dangle from vigorous vinesat Castle Howard in York, England.

White Cup and Saucer Vine
(*Cobaea scandens* 'Alba')

Cup and saucer vine is grown for its charming violet-colored blossoms, but this cultivar, 'Alba', has lightly fragrant white flowers, making it a great addition to the evening garden. If you have a spot that calls for a fast-growing annual vine, this might be the answer. In its tropical native habits, it becomes a woody perennial vine, and bats pollinate the flowers at night. In colder climates, sow seeds outdoors after the last frost date in spring. Or get a head start by sowing seeds indoors a few weeks earlier.

COMMON NAMES: cup and saucer vine, cathedral bells; HARDINESS: annual (zones 9 to 11); SIZE: 10-15 feet; climbs by twining; CONDITIONS: full sun and rich, moist, well-drained soil; CARE: amend the soil with organic matter before sowing seeds; PLANT PARTNERS: corkscrew vine, morning glories, purple hyacinth bean; NOTES: native to Mexico and tropical South America.

Chapter 10

Bulbs: Early, Middle, and Late Bloomers

One of the loveliest white gardens I've ever experienced was that of my friend Lynne in Joliet, Illinois. Outside the tall living room windows of her 1920s-era storybook Tudor home she had a romantic, white-flowered garden planted in the shade of a century-old maple. The garden kicked off in spring with a multitude of white daffodils, crocus, tulips, hyacinths, and spring beauties, followed by ferns, silver-spotted lungwort (*Pulmonaria*), and large drifts of Annabelle hydrangeas. A small bench, a few stone steppers, and a birdbath rounded out the scene. It was a lovely place to sit in the shade during the summer and in the evening as well.

There's no need to limit your white garden to only the summer months. You can plan it for bloom beginning in spring with bulbs, followed by spring-blooming perennials, summer-flowering bulbs and annuals, and by late-season perennials and shrubs. It becomes a multi-season theme garden in sun or shade.

Our garden features many white-flowered daffodils that begin in March and are followed by others that bloom in April and May. Spring-blooming bulbs are especially helpful in shady spots where they can provide early season color before the trees leaf out.

Spring-blooming bulbs extend the season in the white garden.

Plan for a succession of color with bulbs.

Bulbs, Corms, and More

Some plants store all the food they need to grow in a little underground package. For the sake of simplicity, they are often called bulbs. However, this group includes plants that grow from true bulbs, corms, tubers, tuber-corms, tuberous roots, and rhizomes. A true bulb is an enlarged, modified bud. Inside it contains a short vertical stem surrounded by scalelike leaves that hold stored food. Some examples are daffodils, lilies, tulips, and alliums.

A true bulb is a large, modified bud.

Crocus, trout lily (*Erythronium*), *Gladiolus*, *Freesia*, and *Liatris* grow from corms, a solid vertical stem with a bud at the top. Corms are annual structures that store all the food needed to produce flowers and leaves. During the growing season, new corms develop underground from lateral buds. They have roots that pull the new corms down into the soil as the old one shrivels and dies.

While many bulbs and corms are winter hardy and can survive very cold temperatures, some are not. The very fragrant tuberose is an example. In colder regions once the leaves and flowers have been touched by frost, the bulbs can be dug up and saved indoors. Shake off the soil clinging to the roots and cut off all the foliage 1 to 2 inches above the top of the bulbs. Let them dry for a few days in a place that's in shade and out of the rain. Store them over winter indoors in slightly moistened peat moss or vermiculite. A cool, dry spot like a basement or garage that does not freeze will do. Check the bulbs occasionally so that they're not too dry or too wet, which can cause mold.

A rhizome is an enlarged horizontal stem that grows at or just below the soil surface where they form roots from the bottom and send shoots upward. Rhizomes store the plant's nutrients for the following growing season. Canna lilies, calla lilies, and bearded iris are examples of plants that grow from rhizomes. Rhizomatous plants are typically hardy in cold climates.

Corms store food for the above-ground plant.

Tubers form from a stem or root and have nodes (like the eyes on a potato). They also store nutrients. Unlike a bulb, new stems grow upward from many different places on the tuber.

Dahlias and daylilies grow from tuberous roots, a swollen root structure that stores the plant's food. Tiny feeder roots take in nutrients to feed the plant. A dahlia's tuberous roots are generally planted right below the soil surface.

Spring-blooming bulbs are winter-hardy in most Northern states. You plant them in the fall for bloom the following spring. After that, they go dormant until the following year with the leaves dying down once the flowers are finished. Unless the plants are crowded after many years, they don't need dividing.

Summer-blooming bulbs (and some corms and rhizomes) are not winter hardy. You plant them in the spring, and they grow and bloom in summer. They can either be treated like annuals or you can dig them up and store them indoors over the winter for replanting the following spring. Some examples of summer bulbs are dahlias, cannas, gladiolas, and tuberous begonias.

Here's a look at some popular spring- and summer-blooming plants to add to your white garden.

Dahlias grow from tubers. .

Snowdrops are one of the earliest bulbs to bloom in cold-weather climates.

Snowdrops (*Galanthus spp.*)

Snowdrops are one of the first flowers that appear in our garden in mid to late winter. As their name implies, they sometimes pop up through newly fallen snow with their sweet, nodding flowers. Snowdrops work well beneath deciduous trees or shrubs. Their foliage is short, so shade-loving perennials can cover the spent leaves as spring progresses. Plant snowdrops in large numbers (a dozen or more) in a circle for impact. If they like where they're planted, they sometimes reseed, a delightful addition to the white garden.

COMMON NAMES: snowdrops, candlemas bells; **HARDINESS:** zones 4 or 5 depending on species; **SIZE:** most are 3 to 9 inches tall, but giant snowdrops (G. elwesii) can reach 11 inches; **CONDITIONS:** full sun in light, rich soil; **CARE:** plant bulbs in fall in a sandy-loamy soil and mulch with compost; **PLANT PARTNERS:** hostas, hellebores, epimedium, native woodland wildflowers, other shade-loving plants; **NOTES:** snowdrops may be left to form large, densely packed colonies.

Dahlias (*Dahlia*)

Dahlia flowers can be tiny, tight blossoms an inch or two wide or they can be as large as a dinner plate. Depending on the cultivar, the leaves may be a glossy green or rich, burgundy brown. Dahlias grow from tuberous roots and many of them originated in the uplands of Mexico and Guatemala.

On his farm west of Chicago, my friend Dean grows more than 300 hundred dahlias, including the 6-foot-tall 'Peaches 'nCream' that won him a first prize at a dahlia exhibition. Each fall when frost descends, he digs the plants, cuts off the foliage, and stores the tubers in onion bags, each marked with its cultivar name. The time and effort are worth it, providing thousands of blooms each summer. There are many white-flowered daffodils available in a wide range of flower sizes. Try a few!

From tiny to the size of dinner plates, there are many white and pale yellow dahlias from which to choose.

COMMON NAMES: dahlia; **HARDINESS:** zone 9; **SIZE:** from dwarf, low-growing plants to 3 to 6 foot plants; **CONDITIONS:** full sun, rich, well-drained soil; **CARE:** plant tubers outdoors as soon as any chance of spring frost has passed; **PLANT PARTNERS:** other white-flowering annuals; **NOTES:** In areas with killing fall frosts, dig up roots in autumn, cut off foliage, shake off soil and dry the tuberous roots in the sun for a few hours. Cover roots with lightly moist sand or vermiculite and store in a cool place until spring.

Daffodils (*Narcissus*)

The most popular spring-blooming bulb has to be the daffodil. *Narcissus* is the botanical name for all daffodils. Jonquils are a type of daffodil characterized by several yellow flowers, strong scent, and rounded foliage. One of the nice things about planting daffodil bulbs is that they return each year, and the bulbs are usually left alone by squirrels or other rodents. (They may dig them up, but they won't eat them!)

Daffodils are easy to grow and most bloom for several weeks. They are quite cold-hardy and often recover from a layer of snow. Except for parts of Florida that are frost-free, daffodils can be grown throughout the United States where there are periods of cold weather. Cold is needed to induce flower bud formation.

In warm parts of the country, wait to plant bulbs in the fall until the soil has cooled to less than 70 F. Follow the planting instructions on the package. Generally, daffodil bulbs are planted 1½ times as deep as the depth of the bulb. Planting too shallow may cause the bulb to split prematurely, producing many small, nonflowering offshoots.

By choosing early, mid, and, late spring daffodil cultivars, you can have three months of flowers.

The heirloom daffodil 'Thalia' offers dainty spring flowers.

COMMON NAMES: jonquil, daffodil; **HARDINESS:** zones 4 to 7 depending on cultivar; **SIZE:** from 6 to 18 inches tall depending on cultivar; **CONDITIONS:** full to part sun in well-drained soil enriched with compost; plant bulbs in fall allowing at least a month for root development before soil freezes; **CARE:** leave dried leaves intact until they can be gently pulled away; **PLANT PARTNERS:** other spring-blooming bulbs; **NOTES:** bulbs will rot in soggy, water-logged soil.

Tulips (*Tulipa*)

Some of my favorite tulips are the peony-flowered types like 'Mount Tacoma' and 'Danceline' with their large, double white flowers on long stems. There's the lily-flowered 'White Triumphator', introduced about 1942 with its pure white flowers on 24-inch stems. But my all-time favorite is 'Maureen' for its enormous, oval-shaped flowers that open as a very pale yellow and mature to a glistening white.

Plant in late fall in well-drained, sandy, humus-rich soil. Packages may recommend planting bulbs 4 to 8 inches deep. When planted deeper (12 inches) bulbs will multiply less quickly but may last longer, producing blooms for many years. Tulips prefer dry conditions during the summer months. Some gardeners treat tulips as annuals and plant new bulbs each fall. In an area next to our home's foundation, the soil tends to be quite dry and that is a spot where tulips have persisted for several years. Beware that mice and chipmunks are fond of the bulbs.

Tulips do best in soils that are allowed to dry in summer months.

COMMON NAMES: tulips; **HARDINESS:** zones 4 to 5; **SIZE:** from 6 to 20 inches; **CONDITIONS:** dry, rich soil in full sun; **CARE:** do not remove the leaves until they turn yellow; **PLANT PARTNERS:** daffodils, crocus, hyacinths; **NOTES:** plant bulbs in an area that will not require watering in summer.

Tulips add an elegant touch to the white garden in spring.

Spring crocus flaunt their flowers.

Dutch Crocus (*Crocus vernus*)

These sweet little flowers appear in early spring to carpet the ground with white, yellow, or pale lilac flowers. A beautiful cultivar is 'Jeanne D'arc' (aka 'Joan of Arc') with large upright, pure-white flowers. Plant the corms in fall in a place where you can enjoy the low-growing blossoms. Interplant them with short, early blooming daffodils like 'Thalia', 'Ice Wings', or 'Snow Baby'. Although most crocus species hail from regions with intense summer heat, they usually need winter cold to thrive.

COMMON NAMES: crocus, dutch crocus, spring crocus; **HARDINESS:** zone 4; **SIZE:** 2 to 8 inches tall; **CONDITIONS:** full sun, well-drained rich soil; **CARE:** let the foliage die back before removing if needed; **PLANT PARTNERS:** other spring-blooming bulbs, shade plants; **NOTES:** amend the soil before planting.

Gladiolus (*Gladiolus*)

I sometimes think of "glads" as funeral flowers because they often appear in arrangements at wakes. However, these wonderful heirloom plants deserve a place in the white garden, and I often see them sold as cut flowers at the local farmer's market. They are grown from corms and are best grown in moist, humus-rich soil in full sun. Because the flower stalks are quite tall, I plant them in spots out of the wind.

COMMON NAMES: gladiola, gladiolus, gladioli; **HARDINESS:** zones 7 to 10; **SIZE:** 1½ to 4 feet tall; **CONDITIONS:** full sun in fertile, moist, well-drained soil; **CARE:** plant corms 4 to 6 inches deep and provide consistent moisture; **PLANT PARTNERS:** annuals, such as white-flowered cosmos, zinnias, and dahlias; **NOTES:** after foliage yellows, dig the corms (and cormels—small offshoots), cut off the dried leaves and store the corms in a cool, frost-free spot indoors.

The upright flowers of gladiolus provide a vertical accent in the garden.

Ornamental Onion (*Allium giganteum*)

The large, ball-shaped flowers of ornamental onions seem to float over other plants in our spring garden. Although many produce violet or purple flowers, there are several white cultivars such as 'Mount Everest', a tall variety with baseball-size, glistening white flowers heads. Alliums are available in many species, cultivars, and sizes from 6 inches to 4 feet tall. I like the giant, ornamental onions with their great flower heads for that wow factor in late spring. They make a long-lasting cut flower, too.

COMMON NAMES: ornamental onion; **HARDINESS:** zones 4 to 10; **SIZE:** 1 to 3 feet depending on cultivar; **CONDITIONS:** full sun, well-drained soil; **CARE:** plant bulbs in fall; **PLANT PARTNERS:** choose sun-loving perennials that will cover the spent leaves; **NOTES:** yellowing leaves should be left on plants until dry and then removed.

White ornamental onions provide a "wow" factor.

Summer snowflake's delicate, nodding flowers add grace to the garden.

Summer Snowflake (*Leucojum aestivum*)

One of my favorite flowers is summer snowflake with its bell-shaped delicate white flowers. A native of England, summer snowflake dates back to 1594. The cultivar 'Gravetye Giant' is a 1920s hybrid with very large, white flowers tipped with pale green. Plants bloom for about three weeks in our garden, where they mingle with perennial geraniums. In areas of dappled sunlight, they can slowly naturalize to create lovely clumps. The blossoms also make nice flower arrangements if you can bear to cut them.

COMMON NAMES: summer snowflake, snowflake; **HARDINESS:** zones 4 to 9; **SIZE:** 12 to 24 inches tall; **CONDITIONS:** moist, well-drained soil in dappled bright light; **CARE:** when finished blooming, let the leaves remain in place; **PLANT PARTNERS:** early summer bloomers like perennial geraniums, ornamental onions; **NOTES:** deer- and rodent-resistant.

Lilies (*Lilium*)

A white evening garden wouldn't be complete without the extremely showy flowers of lilies. There are more than 80 known species and countless cultivars, with some native to the United States. Lilies prefer a light, loamy soil with an organic mulch and good drainage. Most like full sun, but some benefit from part shade in the afternoon. The 3- to 4-foot-tall cultivar, 'Casa Blanca', is one of my favorites for its large, fragrant flowers that appear in mid to late summer, not long after our Asiatic lilies. Both types of lilies are easy to grow and many are hardy to Zone 4, but some are tender plants, like *L. longiflorum*, often called Easter lilies because they are sold during that holiday. Plant lilies so that their roots are kept cool and in the shade. Mulching will help but don't pile mulch on plant stems.

'Casa Blanca' lily is a visual stunner and fragrant, too.

COMMON NAMES: asiatic lily, madonna lily, fragrant lily; **HARDINESS:** zones 4 to 9 depending on species or cultivar; **SIZE:** 2 to 6 feet; **CONDITIONS:** full sun to part shade; average well-drained soil; **CARE:** lilies like their "heads" in the sun and the roots in shade; **PLANT PARTNERS:** daylilies, ornamental onions, dahlias, iris; **NOTES:** plant bulbs in groups of three or five for a good display.

Bearded irises offer giant blooms over a period of weeks.

Iris (*Iris*)

There are about 300 species of iris, some of which grow from rhizomes that grow close to or directly under the soil surface. A favorite is the bearded iris with its fans of sword-shaped leaves and beautiful blossoms, and the trouble-free Siberian iris with its small flowers on compact plants. Most flower in spring or early summer. Some irises, like the tiny spring-blooming *Iris reticulata* grow from bulbs. Depending on the species or cultivar, they can be anywhere from 3 inches to 4 feet tall or more.

COMMON NAMES: iris, bearded iris, Sberian iris; **HARDINESS:** zones 2 to 9 depending on species or cultivar; **SIZE:** 3 inches to 4 feet tall or more; **CONDITIONS:** full sun to part shade; well-drained soil; **CARE:** bearded iris rhizomes should be planted at the soil surface or just below; **PLANT PARTNERS:** roses, peonies, catmint; **NOTES:** let the spent flowers and foliage remain on plants until totally dry.

Chapter 11

Exotics, Tropicals, and More Night-Bloomers

Previous chapters feature some plants, like tobacco flower (*Nicotiana sylvestris*) that offer a more pronounced fragrance after dusk. But there are a few others that don't fall neatly into any particular category. Those featured here may be grown as houseplants. My jasmine vines come indoors in October before the first fall frost and then go back outside in May after the last spring frost.

Then there are white-flowered water lilies that can be grown in a large tub outdoors if you don't have the space for a pond. There are many indoor plants that can do double-duty, enhancing your outdoor spaces during the growing season. Here's a look at a few sensational (and unusual) plants for your white garden.

White *Cyclamen persicum* in a pot enhances indoor spaces with its unique upswept petals and heart-shaped leaves.

Indoor potted plants like this Kalanchoe can accessorize your white garden in summer.

Evening Rain Lily
(*Zephyranthes drummondii*)

A native plant that hails from the prairies and meadows of western and south central United States, rain lily has fragrant white flowers that open in the evening. Some of these areas have intermittent rain and dry spells, thus its name refers to when the plant flowers—after a rainfall, especially in late summer. The flowers last a few days and gradually fade to pink. Plants are grown from bulbs and the best flowering is in full sun. They are hardy in Zones 7b through 10a, so if you live in a colder area, you may want to dig the bulbs and overwinter them indoors. They can also be grown in containers.

COMMON NAMES: evening rain lily, giant rain lily, prairie lily; **HARDINESS:** zones 7 to 10; **SIZE:** 6 to 12 inches tall and wide; **CONDITIONS:** full sun and moist to dry garden soil; **CARE:** tolerates sandy, loamy soil that is well-drained; **PLANT PARTNERS:** coneflowers, shasta daisies, liatris; **NOTES:** flowers gradually open in the evening after rainfall.

A rain lily's fragrant flowers open at night.

Night-blooming cereus flowers are short-lived but spectacular.

Queen of the Night Cereus
(*Epiphyllum oxypetalum*)

This magical night-bloomer boasts showy, fragrant, white flowers that close up at dawn. A member of the cactus family, it grows in rainforests and is considered a tropical cactus. In its native habitat (Southern Mexico and Central America), the plants grow on trees, but they are easily grown in containers as a houseplant that vacations outdoors in summer. Plants prefer a potting mix geared to succulents and cactus.

COMMON NAMES: night-blooming cereus, orchid cactus, queen of the night; **HARDINESS:** zones 10 to 11; **SIZE:** in frost-free climates, plants can grow 8 to 10 feet tall and 3 feet wide; in colder climates plants are grown in containers and wintered indoors; **CONDITIONS:** part shade or indirect bright light; let the top inch or two of soil dry between waterings; **CARE:** reduce watering when wintering plants indoors; **PLANT PARTNERS:** grown alone in a pot; **NOTES:** soak the soil until the water runs into the saucer and then empty the excess water.

Jasmine (*Jasminum polyanthum*)

There are many plants that are lumped under the name "jasmine", but this one, native to China, offers a sweet, honey-scented fragrance that can fill a room or a white garden during the warm months. It can be grown in a pot and placed in a bed or border among other white flowers, or plant it in the ground in frost-free areas and let it scramble up a trellis.

COMMON NAMES: jasmine, pink jasmine, winter jasmine; **HARDINESS:** zones 8 to 11; **SIZE:** in frost-free climates, the vines can reach 20 to 25 feet; **CONDITIONS:** full sun to part shade; place containers in sheltered, frost-free areas; **CARE:** keep soil moist but not soggy; **PLANT PARTNERS:** clematis, roses; **NOTES:** offers a long bloom season.

Jasmine's tiny, star-shaped blossoms offer a delicate fragrance on warm evenings.

The fragrance of common jasmine spills into the garden at dusk.

Common Jasmine (*Jasminum officinale*)

This jasmine species, often called "common jasmine," is a twining deciduous shrub that can perfume an entire garden with its lovely fragrance. In warm climates (zones 7 and higher), the plants are perennial. In colder situations (zone 8 and further north), they can be grown in containers to add fragrance to a bed, border, deck, or patio. Plants bloom for many weeks.

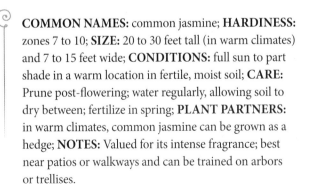

COMMON NAMES: common jasmine; **HARDINESS:** zones 7 to 10; **SIZE:** 20 to 30 feet tall (in warm climates) and 7 to 15 feet wide; **CONDITIONS:** full sun to part shade in a warm location in fertile, moist soil; **CARE:** Prune post-flowering; water regularly, allowing soil to dry between; fertilize in spring; **PLANT PARTNERS:** in warm climates, common jasmine can be grown as a hedge; **NOTES:** Valued for its intense fragrance; best near patios or walkways and can be trained on arbors or trellises.

Star Jasmine
(*Trachelospermum jasminoides*)

Star jasmine is a twining plant that is a woody perennial in mild climates like Southern California and in the Southwest and Southeast United States. Although it's not a true jasmine, it has creamy white flowers that emit a sweet fragrance from late spring into early summer with sporadic blooms through fall.

COMMON NAMES: star jasmine; **HARDINESS:** zones 8 to 10; **SIZE:** 3 to 6 feet tall and wide; **CONDITIONS:** part shade and medium-wet, well-drained loamy soils; **CARE:** in cold climates it can be grown as a container plant and overwintered indoors; **PLANT PARTNERS:** grow it alone as a shrub or ground cover in mild climates; **NOTES:** may be grown as an annual in colder climates.

Star jasmine offers weeks of fragrant white blossoms.

Evening primroses range in color from pale yellow and gold to pure white.

Common Evening Primrose
(*Oenothera biennis*)

Evening primroses are native to North America and some parts of South America. Bowl-shaped fragrant flowers start out a pale yellow and age to a dark golden yellow. There are others that bloom white or pink and many are fragrant. They open in the evening from summer to fall. If plants like the location, they may self-sow and you'll have an ongoing display every year. There are other species as well. 'Greencourt Lemon' Missouri or Ozark sundrops (*Oenothera macrocarpa* 'Greencourt Lemon') is one of many cultivars with very pale-yellow flowers that can reach 5 inches across.

COMMON NAMES: evening primrose, sundrops; **HARDINESS:** zones 4 to 8; **SIZE:** 6 inches tall to 20 inches across depending on species and cultivar; **CONDITIONS:** full sun and dry soil; **CARE:** remove unwanted seedlings in spring; wet soils can lead to root rot; **PLANT PARTNERS:** liatris, lilies, daylilies; **NOTES:** Ozark primrose is a vigorous perennial and can be aggressive.

Try growing a native white water lily in a tub or small pond.

American White Water Lily (*Nymphaea odorata*)

One of the most common waterlilies, this one is native to the Northeastern United States and parts of Canada. The flowers and leaves float on the water, but you don't need a pond or a giant water feature. You can grow water lilies in a tub outdoors. Flowers can be 6 to 9 inches wide. Grab a cup of coffee or tea in the morning and sit outside to enjoy them—plants usually flower from early morning until noon and you won't want to miss it.

COMMON NAMES: fragrant white water lily; **HARDINESS:** zones 4 to 11; **SIZE:** 2 to 12 inches tall and 2 to 4 feet wide; can form dense colonies; **CONDITIONS:** full to part sun; **CARE:** plant rhizomes in containers, cover with soil and place the top of the pots within 6 to 8 inches below the water's surface; **PLANT PARTNERS:** other aquatic plants grown in pots, like canna lilies; **NOTES:** for the best flowering provide a large water garden in full sun.

Angel's Trumpet (*Brugmansia spp.*)

Angel's trumpets are valued for their large, usually scented trumpet-shaped flowers that appear from late spring to autumn. In mild areas, they can be grown as specimen plants, but they are not hardy in colder climates. They can be grown in containers and moved outdoors in summer.

COMMON NAMES: angel's trumpet, angels' trumpets; **HARDINESS:** zones 8 to 10; **SIZE:** can get to be 8 feet tall or larger without pruning; **CONDITIONS:** full sun, enriched soil or potting mix; **CARE:** full sun and fertile, moist, well-drained soil; **PLANT PARTNERS:** best grown alone and in a pot in cooler climates; **NOTES:** all parts are toxic if ingested.

One of the most exotic plants for the white garden, angel's trumpet has spectacular downward-facing blossoms.

Four-O'Clocks (*Mirabalis jalapa*)

Here's a plant that tells time. Well, sort of. The name four-o'clocks refers to the fragrant flowers that open in the late afternoon. Flower colors include pink, rose, red, magenta, yellow, and white, and several flower colors may be present on one plant. However, there are white-flowered varieties that you can grow from seed as well.

COMMON NAMES: four o'clocks, marvel of peru; **HARDINESS:** zones 9 to11; **SIZE:** 24 to 30 inches tall and wide; **CONDITIONS:** full sun to part shade, well-drained moist soil; **CARE:** plants may be grown as tender perennials in zones 7 to 9; elsewhere grown as an annual; **PLANT PARTNERS:** pair with other white-flowered annuals; **NOTES:** attracts butterflies and birds.

White-flowered four-o'clocks open their blossoms in late afternoon.

Tuberose (*Polianthes tuberosa*)

One of the most fragrant plants in our garden is the tuberose. When I was a teenager, my mum grew this plant in our backyard, and I would pop a flower or two into my long hair on a summer's eve. This tender perennial (an annual in our zone 5 garden) grows from tuberous rhizomes and produces lance-shaped leaves topped with spikes of intensely fragrant waxy white flowers. The cultivar 'The Pearl' bears semi-double flowers. The plants hail from Mexico and require a minimum temperature of 59° F. The tubers may be overwintered indoors.

One of the most fragrant flowers, tuberose is a must for the white garden.

COMMON NAMES: tuberose; **HARDINESS:** zones 7 to 10; **SIZE:** 2 to 3 feet tall and 2 feet wide; **CONDITIONS:** rich, well-drained soil, medium moisture and full sun; **CARE:** plant roots about 2 inches deep in spring after the last frost date; provide consistent moisture; **PLANT PARTNERS:** best grown in groups near patios, walks, decks or containers where the fragrance can be enjoyed; **NOTES:** lift tuberous rhizomes after the leaves die and once they are dry, store them in peat or vermiculite in a frost-free place over winter.

Night-scented Stock
(*Matthiola longipetala*)

Although night-scented stock isn't necessarily a "wow" plant during the day, its tiny flowers release an intoxicating fragrance at dusk. My grandfather sent seeds of this annual from England to Chicago to my homesick mother who loved the scent. This lovely heirloom can be used in beds, borders, and containers where it makes a lovely contribution to the evening garden. They can be grown from seed and may occasionally self-sow.

COMMON NAMES: night-scented stock; evening-scented stock; **HARDINESS:** hardy annual; **SIZE:** 1 foot tall and 6 inches wide; **CONDITIONS:** full sun to part shade with well-drained soil; **CARE:** water regularly while plants are established; **PLANT PARTNERS:** plant with other annual flowers; **NOTES:** mix in compost before transplanting or sowing seeds.

A favorite of Victorian gardeners, night-scented stock is a delight at night.

The North American native perennial prospers in moist soil.

Nodding Ladies' Tresses
(*Spiranthes cernua*)

If you have a wet or moist area in your white garden, this cheery North American native may be for you. It produces white spires of delicate flowers from late summer into autumn. The low rosette of silvery green leaves are topped with pure white blossoms that last for several weeks in cool autumn weather. Over time, the plant can form small colonies with tuberous roots.

COMMON NAMES: nodding ladies' tresses, fragrant ladies' tresses; **HARDINESS:** zones 4 to 8; **SIZE:** 1 to 2 feet tall and 3 to 12 inches wide; **CONDITIONS:** part to full shade; moist soil; **CARE:** site plants in an area with moist, damp soil; **PLANT PARTNERS:** other perennials that tolerate moist soil; **NOTES:** incorporate compost into the soil before planting.

Index

Note: Page numbers in *italics* indicate/include photo captions. Page numbers in **bold** indicate plant specie summaries.

Photo Credits

Alamy.com

Page 29: *top* Stephen Chung, *bottom* PA Images; page 30: Amanda Rose; page 43: micboss/Stockimo

Shutterstock.com

Pages 2–4: mrs_kato; page 8: *bottom left* Alex Alexandrov, *header background* mrs_kato; page 9: left Uladzik Kryhin; page 10: *top* Alla Tsyganova; page 16: *bottom* gizem elibol; page 40: *header background* mrs_kato; page 43: *top* rieffmicrostock; page 51 & 52: *striped background* mrs_kato; page 53: *bottom* Joseph Hendrickson; page 61: *left* HY-DP, *right* PTCH; page 62: *top* Chris Mann; page 66: *top* Stenko Vlad; page 67: mrs_kato, Alexey Stiop; page 68: mrs_kato; page 75: mrs_kato; page 76: *striped background* mrs_kato; page 90: *striped background* mrs_kato; page 100: *striped background* mrs_kato; *striped background* page 112: *striped background* mrs_kato; page 114: *top* Inna Shport; page 122: *striped background* mrs_kato; page 126: *bottom* ChunPicture; page 127: *bottom* TRR, joojoob27; page 128: *top* Irina Starikova1811; page 129: *top* Svetlana Mahovskaya; page 132: *striped background* mrs_kato; page 140: *striped background* mrs_kato; page 142: *top* Mircea Moira; page 143: *bottom* Totokzww; page 144: *top* APugach, *bottom* Konstantinos Livadas; page 146: *top* Sarawut Pr; page 147: *top* yakonstant, *bottom* RasaBasa.

The author thanks the following for sharing images of their projects and plants: Anna Bagliore, Ferry-Morse; Diane Blazek, National Garden Bureau; Dale Deppe, Spring Meadow Nursery; Roy Diblik, Northwind Perennial Farm; Mark Dwyer, Landscape Prescriptions by MD; Galen Gates, Horticultural Consultant; Alastair Gunn, Castle Howard, England; Hans Hansen, Walter's Gardens; Rita Hassert, The Morton Arboretum; Bob Hursthouse, Hursthouse, Inc.; Dan Kennedy, Logee's Plants for Home & Garden; Benjamin Lenhardt, Jr., The Garden Conservancy; Ashley Marrin, Bret-Mar Landscaping; Greg Moroz, Sunny's Garden; Marya Padour, Camp Rosemary; Avery Pronschinske, Olbrich Botanical Gardens; Becky Starovich, Rosborough Partners, Inc.; Rotary Botanical Gardens, Janesville, WI; Katie Rotella, The Gardens at Ball; Jeanine Standard, Proven Winners; and John Sullivan, Sully's Garden.

All other photos submitted by the author, except where otherwise noted.

About the Author

An award-winning gardening expert, Nina Koziol has been an adjunct faculty member at the Chicago Botanic Garden and an instructor at The Morton Arboretum since 1998. She is a frequent writer and contributor for Chicago Botanic Garden's website, and she has also written for *Aquascape Lifestyles*, *Organic Gardening*, *Chicagoland Gardening*, *Old House Journal*, *Fine Gardening*, *Country Garden*, and *The American Gardener*. From 1995 to 2016, Nina was a garden writer and contest judge for the *Chicago Tribune*, and she currently writes for Illinois Landscape Contractors Association's *The Landscape Contractor* magazine and teaches educational classes at their annual conference. The Garden Writers of America (now GardenComm) awarded Nina "Musings of an Everyday Gardener" in the *Chicago Tribune*'s Home & Garden section. She has also presented a variety of programs for the Illinois State Master Gardener conference, the Perennial Plant Association, and other organizations.